I Run, Therefore I Am STILL Nuts!

Bob Schwartz

Illustrated by
B.K. Taylor

Library of Congress Cataloging-in-Publication Data

Schwartz, Bob, 1960-
  I run, therefore I am STILL nuts! / Bob Schwartz.
    p. cm.
  1. Running--Humor. I. Title.
  PN6231.R85S38 2012
  818'.602--dc23

                            2012021307

ISBN-10: 1-4504-2856-8 (print)
ISBN-13: 978-1-4504-2856-9 (print)

The web addresses cited in this text were current as of May 2012, unless otherwise noted.

Acquisitions Editor: Tom Heine; **Developmental Editor:** Anne Hall; **Assistant Editor:** Tyler M. Wolpert; **Copyeditor:** Annette Pierce; **Permissions Manager:** Martha Gullo; **Graphic Designer:** Fred Starbird; **Graphic Artist:** Tara Welsch; **Cover Designer:** Keith Blomberg; **Art Manager:** Kelly Hendren; **Associate Art Manager:** Alan L. Wilborn; **Illustrations (cover and interior):** © B.K. Taylor; **Printer:** United Graphics

Human Kinetics books are available at special discounts for bulk purchase. Special editions or book excerpts can also be created to specification. For details, contact the Special Sales Manager at Human Kinetics.

Printed in the United States of America   10 9 8 7 6 5 4 3 2 1

Human Kinetics
Website: www.HumanKinetics.com

United States: Human Kinetics
P.O. Box 5076
Champaign, IL 61825-5076
800-747-4457
e-mail: humank@hkusa.com

Canada: Human Kinetics
475 Devonshire Road Unit 100
Windsor, ON N8Y 2L5
800-465-7301 (in Canada only)
e-mail: info@hkcanada.com

Europe: Human Kinetics
107 Bradford Road
Stanningley
Leeds LS28 6AT, United Kingdom
+44 (0) 113 255 5665
e-mail: hk@hkeurope.com

Australia: Human Kinetics
57A Price Avenue
Lower Mitcham, South Australia 5062
08 8372 0999
e-mail: info@hkaustralia.com

New Zealand: Human Kinetics
P.O. Box 80
Torrens Park, South Australia 5062
0800 222 062
e-mail: info@hknewzealand.com

E5708

As always, the essence of everything in my life comes back to my wife, Robin. Through success, through failure, through ongoing laughter, and through occasional tears, she has been my source of indescribable happiness. Her delicate balance of kindness, strength, intelligence, and compassion produces the greatest friend imaginable.

Thanks, my love.

Contents

Part X   The Legs Have It! Don't Be Defeeted   195

Figuring Out What Will Keep You on the Streets

Part XI   Behind Every Runner Are Very Accepting Nonrunners   213

The Runner's Family Knows Their RICE From Their DOMS

Acknowledgments

There's something to be said for persistence, and I'd be remiss if I didn't first acknowledge the gentle persistence of Human Kinetics Acquisitions Editor Tom Heine. Over the course of a few years, Tom would, from time to time, politely attempt to persuade me to write a sequel to *I Run, Therefore I Am—NUTS!* For various reasons I was not in a position to devote the time and energy required for writing a sequel. Eventually, the timing became better and I agreed. In the end, Tom couldn't have been more correct and I couldn't have been happier. A certain joy emanates from doing what you love, and humorously writing about my passion for running is my writer's high. So thanks to Tom for his foresight, his vision, and his patience with me in getting this book accomplished.

As with the first book, tremendous gratitude is owed to my good friend and illustrator, B.K. Taylor, whose sensational artistic talent is matched only by his keen sense of humor. One of the highlights of putting this book together was our meetings to discuss illustration ideas during which, I'd often be reduced to tears of laughter.

Many thanks to my developmental editor, Anne Hall, for her commitment to the book, her insightful comments and suggestions, and her editing acumen.

Lastly, I must acknowledge runners everywhere. Ten years ago when *I Run, Therefore I Am—NUTS!* was published, I had no idea whether it would be a colossal success or an epic failure. Thankfully, it was the former as the book's humor clearly struck a chord with all types of runners. So to runners everywhere, keep enjoying the miles and keep enjoying the laughs with *I Run, Therefore I Am—STILL Nuts!*

Introduction

It's Staring You Right in the Feet

Just about 10 years ago I was putting the finishing touches on the then untitled manuscript for *I Run, Therefore I Am—NUTS!* Martin Barnard, an acquisitions editor at Human Kinetics had requested that when I submitted the manuscript I should also supply the final title for the book. I'd always figured that once the book was complete, a title would be a rather simple task. How hard could a few more words be after writing more than 55,000 of them for the book? Well, think again, Shakespeare!

Over the next few weeks I'd submit daily a few proposed titles, and all of them were politely but summarily rejected. I not only tested the patience of my editor, but I also challenged his ability to come up with new ways to tactfully tell me that my suggested titles were pretty much abysmal. I haven't set a whole lot of running records, but I'm fairly confident that I still hold the North American Literary Record for most rejected titles at 139. Hey, pitiful or not, a record is a record.

My editor finally indicated that the publisher was going to go in a different direction. Namely, in their direction. Without my input. So be it, I thought. Let's see what their collective brain trust could do.

They soon advised me they wanted to do a humorous take off on the Descartes philosophical quote of "I think, therefore I am." They wanted to see whether I could come up with something along those lines. I thought perfecto; I'm back in the game, still in the mix. Things would be much easier now that I'd been given guidance. Wrong again, though. One word describes this title thing and me: naive. That's French for "Buddy, you don't have a clue."

After a week, the best I came up with was *I Stink, Therefore I Ran!* Or how about *I Hit the Wall, Therefore I'm Spam!* With those wonderful submissions, my editor indicated in no uncertain terms that they'd take it from there. I said, "Good luck."

Days later I woke up early one morning and checked my e-mail from the previous evening and saw a message from my publisher and the subject line said, "Final Title Selection." All right, I thought. They'd come up with something. I was grateful. I was relieved. And then I read it. I was wrong.

Without much of a drum roll, the publisher laid it out that the title would be *I Run, Therefore I Am—NUTS!* My less-than-electrified reaction was that their collective effort produced a title far worse than any of mine. That's even including one of my all-time pathetic titles of *Your Second Wind Is Coming, Put on a Happy Pace!*

I stewed about my disdain for their idea and then went for a Midwestern winter-morning run with the wind chill well below zero. I returned with a frost-laden hat, frozen face, and ice-caked eyelashes. I stiffly walked inside and greeted my wife with a numb thumbs-up through my frosted mitten. My wife, who hadn't heard the proposed title yet, just stared at me with an exasperated shake of her head and pronounced (as she'd done many times before), "You're nuts."

Ah ha! I took that as a compliment. She thereby also confirmed the appropriateness of the publisher's title! Although I'd initially thought the term *nuts* might be offensive to runners, I subsequently learned that nothing could have been further from the truth. After the book officially came out, I was a guest speaker at the Chicago Marathon and had a booth where I signed books and behind me hung a large blowup of the book's amusing cover. Runners came by and said, "What a fantastic title!" "That's me!" "How appropriate." "Yeah, I hear you! Right on." Even significant others would get in on the action and say, "Oh yeah. That's you dear."

It was all validated. The title was indeed perfect. We runners are nuts, in a good way, and happy to be a different breed! We wear black toenails as medals of distinction, use more Vaseline in a week than quintuplets with diaper rash and chapped lips, and try to convince ourselves that a horrifically painful muscle pull that prevents us from even walking is really nothing more than a temporary cramp.

Not much has changed with me in the time since the first book came out. I'm still running and although I may be a bit slower with age, I'm still nuts. I've run through 120-degree heat in Las Vegas and foot-deep snow in my home state of Michigan. I keep going despite being periodically visited by the "Itis" family, as in plantar fasciitis, Achilles tendinitis, hip bursitis, and knee tendinitis. I've become intimately familiar with all forms of nonimpact training modes during forced downtime from running, and I've staged more comebacks in the last decade than I can even possibly remember. I've finally come to grasp the realization that what used to heal in about 18 minutes when I was younger, apparently now takes three months.

I've seen one of my children discover the joy of running, and two others view it as sheer torture. I've witnessed my wife return to running after a brief 22-year hiatus. I've run personal best times and personal worst times and learned to accept (a little bit) maximum effort over race results. I watched and then ultimately accepted the emergence of an entirely new breed of runner who focuses more on socializing and fitness and less on producing extreme nausea and cramps at the end of a tough race or training run. I've concluded that having all five members of my neighborhood running group be injury free at the same time is about as likely as the Boston Marathon making an automatic entry to anyone running a marathon in fewer than six hours.

Most of all, over the last 10 years, I've continued to enjoy the pleasures of running and the sometimes humbling nature of it as well. And along the way, a multitude of humorous subjects emerged. I can now share those laughs with you from topics that include what occurs when your favorite training shoe is abruptly discontinued, the inability to admit that an injury is truly a big one, the issue of competition and getting older, the inherent simplicity of running, running alone versus with others, the concept of schadenfreude, running logs, runner's high, excuses, barefoot running, and the many peculiar talents runners possess.

As I head out the door each morning for a run, I often think of a scene in the movie *City Slickers*. The comedy focuses on Billy Crystal's character, Mitch, being plagued by a midlife crisis. He and his friends attempt to find meaning and purpose in life on a cattle-driving vacation. During the movie Mitch has a conversation with Jack Palance's character, Curly, who is a gruff veteran trail boss. The wisdom imparted by Curly is as follows:

Curly to Mitch: Do you know what the secret of life is?

[Curly holds up one finger]

Curly: This.

Mitch: Your finger?

Curly: One thing. Just one thing. You stick to that and the rest don't mean s***.

Mitch: But, what is the "one thing?"

Curly: That's what you have to find out.

And that's the joy of life for me. I found that "one thing" in the simple act of running. A passion that's now been with me for over 40 years and provides so much pleasure, such bliss, that I could wax philosophical about it for a very long time. But you don't want to hear that. You want lots of laughs and I've got those, so I'll wax humorous instead.

Enjoy! And long may you run.

PART

I

It's All in the Approach to Make Your Runs Beyond Reproach

If It Works, Then Don't Nix It

Much Ado About Something

Style points equal mile points

With much anticipation and excitement I finished my run, went inside, and took off my shoes. The latter I'd done innumerable times before, but this time was different. This was the day of reckoning. After a month of my personal experiment, the results were about to be revealed. I grabbed the tops of my shoes and took a deep breath. As the suspense heightened, I glanced toward my wife and requested, "Drum roll, please."

Before revealing the results and what happened next, let me provide some background. When the focus on running form to avoid injury became more prevalent, I didn't think much about it. My motto was "If it works don't fix it." It was running for gosh sakes; it wasn't a golf swing, tennis stroke, or even a basketball jump shot. I recognized that form was significant for those activities and recalled honing my shot with a continuous recitation of "square your body, elbow in, bend your wrist, fingertip release, and follow through." But running? The only cadence in my head was one foot forward, body to follow.

Oh sure, I had endured my share of injuries over the years, but I had never attributed those to form. Instead, I blamed a violation of one or more of the "too" principles. As in, too many miles, too much speed work, too many fast long runs, or the all-too-common double whammy of too much too soon. All of which were too bad.

But then something happened. One of my running buddies told me his wife had seen me running and asked him whether I were combating an injury because it appeared that I was leading and leaning with the left side of my body and my stride was a bit choppy. The good news was I wasn't injured but, then again, the bad news was I wasn't injured (if that was the form I was exhibiting when healthy). Of course, I quickly dismissed her recount, which led me to the only reasonable conclusion. His wife's vision must lean to the left.

When I ran I felt graceful, fluid, and nimble. Leading and leaning to the left? Really? All I kept hearing was Beyonce's song "Irreplaceable" (To the left, to the left, to the left, to the left). I then realized that after 40 years of running, I'd never actually seen myself run except in an occasional reflection in a storefront window. Sure, I'd seen race photos, but never an actual ongoing examination of my running form. I hadn't paid a lot of attention to how I ran, only that I ran. Maybe my form could and should be tweaked, but, then again, what about many elite runners who run fast despite quirks in their form? Such as Paula Radcliffe running like a bobblehead, or Alberto Salazar's shuffling stride, Kara Goucher's or Meb Keflezighi's heel striking, or Bill Rodgers' arm motion crossing his body. I concluded that was all irrelevant because, guess what, I wasn't elite.

So I read a lot about running form (upper body aligned, tall, and relaxed; shoulders loose with forward lean; shorter stride and quick leg turnover; light landing with midfoot strike; and so on) and decided I'd try to implement these characteristics for a month. Most importantly, I'd concentrate on avoiding my usual heel-striking (which produces an inefficient braking effect and also produces more stress and impact) and aim for the midfoot landing. Hence, my experiment. The proof would be in the pudding or, rather, the substantiation would be in the sole.

After 30 days of concentrating on my foot landing, I examined my soles to see how the midfoot strike had changed my usual wear pattern on the heels of my shoes. Back to "Drum roll, please." I turned my shoes over and all I could say was "What the heck?" I was crushed. My wear pattern was pretty much the same as always! Go figure. Apparently, given my limited attention span, my powers of form concentration were not lasting longer than about the first 600 yards of my runs.

I then took the next step, literally, and underwent video analysis of my running gait at a local sports medicine clinic. I'd get to the bottom of this lean-to-the-left thing. The analysis addressed biomechanical abnormalities that should be corrected to improve performance and efficiency and involved a clinical exam and a treadmill run examining the angulations, strength, and flexibility in my hips, knees, and ankles. It provided information on things below my knee but way over my head with terminology like my Q-angle (I was feeling more obtuse than Q) and ankle equinus (limited upward bending of the ankle joint). The video also examined hip hiking (hitch hiking I knew, but I learned the former was the lifting of the hip and pelvis on one side).

Early in the process I sensed that my belief of being a gracefully efficient runner was about to be shattered. Perhaps I was overly sensitive, but when the professionals performing the exam began raising their eyebrows, whispering to each other, and subtly shaking their heads, I was getting a not-so-subtle clue to their opinion. After the analysis was completed, I was advised I had flexibility and strength imbalances, excessive shoulder and hip lateral rotation, a contralateral hip drop, internal thigh rotation caused by hip weakness, and tight lower back and hip flexors. I also pressed too hard on the ball of my right foot, and I was overpronating, overstriding, and overswinging my right arm. Eventually they were over with my various overs. I couldn't help but then somewhat jokingly say, "Other than that, it's all good right?"

One of them then added, "Oh, plus you lead with your left." Great.

Eventually, I walked away with exercises, stretches, and running drills. Over the next few months I implemented everything and was confident that concentrating on my running form had assisted with my speed, efficiency, and leg discomforts. Shortly thereafter, I was cross-training on the elliptical at the fitness center when my wife came by. She looked at me for a bit and had a slightly quizzical expression as I pounded away, feeling smooth and graceful. The machine and I in harmony. She then said, "Do you know you lead with your left?"

Oy! I wonder whether they can do video gait analysis on an elliptical?

Watch What You Say to Me!

Flattery can come from the strangest places

One of the differences between running and many other sports is its individualistic nature. How successfully you perform depends on you alone, and how hard you're willing to go outside of your comfort zone is self-regulated. Our internal voice tells us when to push it harder, and sometimes an undermining voice arises and tells us to go back to sleep when the alarm clock goes off or to cut a run short. My internal voice often employs reverse psychology by appealing to my nuts running gene and asking, "What would a sane person do?"

But now we have other voices coming at us through what we wear on our wrist. Years ago running watches didn't have much more than a stopwatch function. Want to know how far you went? Get in your car, retrace your route, and track it the old-fashioned odometer way. A little more difficult to measure those narrow single-track trail runs. Eventually, GPS technology emerged and we not only had our distance staring us in the face from our running watch, but our pace as well. But why stop there? We can now get the number of calories burned, elevation chart for our route, and the temperature. We can get our heart rate, mile splits, cadence, and step count. A vibration alarm signals when we've gone off pace. Heck, eventually our watches will probably be able to tell us how many more strides before we should rehydrate or pop an energy gel packet.

I certainly welcome all the magic that running watches can provide. However, there's one addition I can do without. Most of us don't have a reality show with a personal trainer shouting words of encouragement. Nor do we have,

My internal voice often employs reverse psychology by appealing to my nuts running gene and asking, "What would a sane person do?"

on a daily basis, race spectators shouting phrases like "You're looking good." But now we can. Sort of. Running watches have come along containing messages that attempt to put us on a pedestal after our runs. The wizards of watch technology offer words of praise like "Atta boy," or "Job well done," or "Way to go." I recognize that some runners enjoy those accolades from their wrist. Personally, I'm leaning toward the opinion that if I need compliments from a chronometer or tributes from my timepiece, well, I may have other issues.

Does any other aspect of my life provide unsolicited words of praise? Heck, no. What's next? My computer saying, "Nice sentence, Bob! Way to string those humorous metaphors. You da man, Shakespeare!" Or does my car tell me, "That was a heck of a parallel parking job! Nobody does that better than you." I can't imagine my stove top saying, "Nice omelet flip there, Chef Incredible! And the coffee this morning smelled divine."

The last things I'm looking for after a particularly bad run are flattering yet fallacious words, which are about as welcome at that point as learning a course was mismeasured after you'd set a PR. It's like the queen and her mirror in *Snow White*:

"My watch, my watch, on my hand. Who's the fastest in the land?"

"You, my runner, are fastest of them all."

I wouldn't bet on it.

What I need are the words of legendary coach Bill Bowerman when my alarm clock goes off as a chilly rain pounds on my roof and I contemplate going back to sleep. I could use a bright flashing neon sign plastered across my bedroom ceiling with Bill's words "There's no such thing as bad weather, just soft people." And feel free to toss in for good measure "So get your lazy hiney out of bed there you weak little man. *Now!*"

> Or does my car tell me, "That was a heck of a parallel parking job! Nobody does that better than you."

I also could use, in the latter stages of a race, my watch to feed me a double dose of Winston Churchill, such as "Never, never, never give up" and "If you're going through hell, keep going." I don't need pearls of drivel like "Wow, you've just gone 20 miles. Amazing! You're the greatest. The wall may be coming soon. Feel free to jog it in from here or, better yet, just take the sweep bus to the finish."

Running watches also come with an artificial runner that lays down the gauntlet to challenge us to a race. That's more like it: a healthy dose of virtual competition. Add in some trash talking and all the better! Let my watch berate me with "Is that all you got, Wonder Boy?" or "Feel free to pick up the pace anytime now."

What I could also use before a race is to glance down at my watch to see words of wisdom from Steve Prefontaine, such as "I run to see who has the most guts, who can punish himself into exhausting pace, and then at the end, punish himself even more. Somebody may beat me, but they are going to have to bleed to do it." That'll get my heart pumping. I don't need flattering bouquets like "I just love the way your singlet matches your shorts."

Feel free to give me a watch that will tell me after a run, "That wasn't good enough, twinkle toes. Better be ready to push it tomorrow!" It was Prefontaine who also said, "You cannot propel yourself forward by patting yourself on the back."

Or by having your watch do the patting for that matter. Or your computer, car, or stove top.

We Could All Use a Little More Common Dense

Sometimes it's best to "Go Your Own Way"

Having lived for five years in Boulder, I often experienced what others had told me about Colorado: If you don't like the weather, just wait 10 minutes. I went on long runs where I'd begin layered with clothing under overcast skies with wind and frigid temperatures. I'd finish the run wearing shorts and a singlet in warm temps under calm blue skies. My waist seemed to have more layers of excess clothing tied around it than there are energy gel packets strewn on the ground just past mile 20 of a marathon.

Similar to Colorado's weather patterns, training advice can also change very quickly. As more studies arise and expert opinions emerge, it becomes easier to adopt the advice "If you don't like the conclusion, then just wait a little. It'll change." Some of the earlier pearls of training wisdom are now labeled myths, half-truths, or simply misleading. In my running career I've seen more than waffle shoe soles, extra-short shorts, and cotton socks go out of fashion. Stretching, long slow distance runs, the 10 percent rule (increase in miles per week to prevent injury), the causes of muscle soreness, and core training have all been modified over time. Heck, the old daily training philosophy of "no pain, no gain" is now the more temperate approach to training of "no pain, no strain, all gain."

I readily admit I'm no scientist as my school science fair projects weren't much more scholarly than does a basketball bounce higher when fully aired or when totally deflated? Or does ice melt if left out of the freezer and, if so, why? Thus, I relied on the exercise physiologists, the scientists, and the medical researchers to provide their advice regarding training methods and running. But as I kept up to date on the latest literature and studies, I couldn't help but think of singer-songwriter Don Henley's lyric "The more I know, the less I understand." Time-honored training methods were often refuted by new studies or discovered to be unsupported by medical science. Even new studies on the same issues often yielded different conclusions. This was initially disconcerting until I concluded that other runners share my approach, known as *Common Dense.*

Call us crazy, stupid, unorthodox, or unconventional, but if we feel better doing something unsupported or refuted by medical science, then we're going to keep doing it! It may not make scientific sense and others may feel we're acting dense, but so be it. A full cool-down after a workout? Count me in despite the current belief that the simple act of breathing after a run may be a more-than-adequate cool-down. The old static-stretching toe touch before a run is useless and may even be counterproductive? I'll keep on truckin' and I'll keep on touchin'! I may not

> My school science fair projects weren't much more scholarly than does a basketball bounce higher when fully aired or when totally deflated? Or does ice melt if left out of the freezer and, if so, why?

have a physiology PhD or an orthopedic MD, but I can offer a *Common Dense* ID!

Cross-training has little impact on my running? I'll supplement my miles with the elliptical even if the people with the high IQs in white coats tell me it won't prevent running injury or make me faster. Spot training doesn't work, and core training may be completely unnecessary? I'll keep believing and work the abs to avoid the flab, thank you very much. It's all *Common Dense*.

Along these lines, a time-honored tenet of running has been challenged, sending a ripple through the running community. An article by Gina Kolata in the July 18, 2011, issue of the *New York Times* refuted the view that soft running surfaces are better for the overall health of runners. Through interviewing various exercise researchers, Kolata noted that no scientific studies provide *concrete* evidence that running on soft terrain is any better for a runner than running on asphalt or other hard surfaces. In essence, there were no grounds for soft ground.

This is where common dense comes in. Call me a dunce if the experts say otherwise, but I'm going with a not-so-giant leap of logic here and concluding that soft feels better than hard. I'm sticking with gentle terrain whenever possible until treadmill manufacturers begin advertising the benefits of their machine's complete absence of a deck cushioning system and promoting that their belt is harder than rocks. Feel free to tell me my head is full of rocks, but it's all *Common Dense*.

I know how my legs feel after gentle trail running and how they feel after a long run on hard streets. In the manner of the famous quote of Senator Bentsen to Senator Quayle in their vice presidential debate of 1988, "I've run on soft dirt. I know soft dirt. Soft dirt is a friend of mine.

> Call me a dunce if the experts say otherwise, but I'm going with a not-so-giant leap of logic here and concluding that soft feels better than hard.

Concrete, you're no soft dirt." *Common Dense*!

Similarly, the act of stretching has undergone changes over time and challenges to its effectiveness. There's the classic static stretching that begat active stretching, and there are proponents of ballistic stretch-

But don't ever, ever try to come between runners and their bagels! Pasta lovers, unite!

ing, passive stretching, and dynamic stretching. One school of thought is to stretch only after working out, and there's the belief that stretching may not be at all necessary to prevent injury. *Common Dense* says otherwise. Go ahead and tell me I'm crazy, and that scientifically it's really not worth it do classic stretches before a run. I'll tell that you after 40 years of doing them and that with leg and back muscles in the early morning wound tighter than a violin's E string, that first mile would otherwise have me resembling someone moving on stilts. In deep sand. I know it may be an antiquated approach, but that's what good old *Common Dense* tells me as ingrained habits die hard. I'm fully aware of the current thought that a warm-up approach consisting of dynamic stretching (stretching muscles while moving them) may be useful. But the idea of doing lively hamstring lunges, butt kicks, and high knees at 5:00 a.m. while half asleep in the dead of winter on my snowy street isn't something I'd be itching to get outside to do. I know my personal limitations, which *Common Dense* has taught me.

Abdominal crunches don't really work? Been to a gym lately? Right or wrong, *Common Dense* abounds! Also, recent studies, such as the one reported in Kelly Bastone's article "Running on Empty" in the May 2010 issue of *Running Times*, have concluded that forgoing carbohydrate before and during a long run can have beneficial effects. Now we runners do a lot of masochistic things like hill training, repeat 800s, and miles and miles in a single bout. Call us crazy, but no matter what the potential benefits of training in a glycogen depleted condition may be, the choice of a prerun PB&J over, say, half a celery stalk isn't going to be debated too terribly long. *Common Dense!* Hand me that Pop Tart, please.

We're a movement whose time has come. My two cents says when in doubt, just use good old-fashioned *Common Dense*.

CHAPTER

4

HIIT Me With My Best Shot

Better fitness through masochism

The most famous single word in cinematic history is from the movie *Citizen Kane*, where Charles Foster Kane, on his deathbed, utters his final word "Rosebud" as a snow globe falls from his hand, smashing to the ground. It is the mysterious and enigmatic opening line of the movie, and its genesis is not fully revealed until the end. Similarly, if you happen to see someone lying on the floor next to a treadmill while curled up in the fetal position in a pool of sweat, don't be surprised if he or she (like Orson Welles' character in *Citizen Kane*) also mutters a perplexing word as a stopwatch slips from the person's grasp. Not "Rosebud" though, but "Tabata." It's then that the person will usually pass out from exhaustion.

For people unfamiliar with the Tabata method of training, let's just say that I've run up steep and seemingly endless mountain roads at high altitude during my years in Colorado and have done lung-searing fartlek workouts on wood chip trails in Oregon. I've pushed myself at the end of races where it's been highly debatable as to whether vomiting or the finish line would arrive first, and I've finished marathons in a languorous stupor where going an additional .000001 of a mile would have definitely been unobtainable. But those arduous endeavors were absolutely nothing compared to the tremendous depths of fatigue that hit me when I first did Tabata, which I also called *Heart Rate Hell.*

You've heard that you should do most of your training runs at a pace that allows you to carry on a normal conversation? Well, with my newly experienced masochistic workout, you can't talk at all, let alone pantomime or even consciously move your lips. You can't even comprehend why you're doing this voluntarily because your pulse feels like it's about to explode out of your carotid artery. And that's a half hour after you're done.

> You can't even comprehend why you're doing this voluntarily as your pulse feels like it's about to explode out of your carotid artery. And that's a half hour after you're done.

Okay, maybe that's a wee bit of hyperbole, but you get my drift. The fact is we all have different definitions of exhaustive or high-intensity or maximum-output effort, which a Tabata workout requires. Some of us may take that to mean an effort that becomes a near-death experience, while others will just get breathing pretty darn hard. Either way, it's not for the faint of heart (literally and figuratively). Those who've tried the Tabata workout have a clear understanding that if you even mutter that word in a crowded fitness center, some grown adults will shake in their spandex.

The Tabata workout is a form of high-intensity interval training, or HIIT, and was introduced years ago by Izumi Tabata, who tested athletes using a mechanically braked cycle ergometer. A Tabata session consists of 20 seconds of maximum output (about 170 percent of your $\dot{V}O2max$ for what that's worth) followed by 10 seconds of rest and then repeated seven more times without pause for a total of four minutes of intense exercise. Any form of cardiovascular workout will suffice, be it running, cycling, or rowing on a machine. Tabata's conclusion was that one could greatly improve cardiovascular fitness, lose fat, and, most importantly, increase both aerobic and anaerobic systems in these brief four-minute workouts. He determined that this approach was much more effective than a slower but longer workout (which only enhances your aerobic conditioning).

Many of us have found ourselves exhausted and with our hands on our knees at the end of 400-meter track intervals, but trust me, this workout is the difference between a pinprick to the finger and a sledgehammer to your toe. You may initially think the good news is that each interval is over in 20 seconds and the whole workout can be completed in only four minutes. However, it's like a pact with the devil because the fact is, if you want fitness in 240 seconds, well, you're going to have to pay for it.

My Tabata workout didn't actually end in four minutes because I needed to add in the 15 minutes after the workout that I spent lying prone on the floor of the fitness center wondering how I had gotten there in the first place. Next, add in the subsequent 10 minutes I spent attempting to become vertical and trying to recall exactly where the men's locker room was. Last was the half hour standing almost comatose in the shower, while my rapidly pounding heartbeat continued to pound through my skull.

There is actually a scientific term for this latter feeling and called EPOC (excess postexercise oxygen consumption), which is the afterburn, or the increased rate of oxygen intake after a rigorous workout. In essence, your metabolism is boosted as you continue to burn calories for a long time afterward while slowly returning to the state your body was in before the exercise took place. Understand though that your body will never actually ever, ever be in the same state it was pre-Tabata. I felt like I was in a different state in the country from where I began.

With my first attempt at Tabata, I used an elliptical with a digital timer on its display board while also setting the alarm on my watch to beep after 20 seconds and again after 10 seconds. During the first interval I was quickly convinced my watch had malfunctioned and the alarm hadn't gone off properly. I glanced down at the display board and saw that I'd been at it for a measly 9 seconds! My first 20 seconds of full-bore effort seemed to have lasted longer than listening to the full, eight-minute version of Led Zeppelin's "Stairway to Heaven." Time didn't just stand still; it felt like it was going backward. I'll let you in on a little secret regarding the subsequent 10-second rest period. That period will pass as quickly as the time it takes you to read this word: moron.

> I'll let you in on a little secret regarding the subsequent 10-second rest period. That period will pass as quickly as the time it takes you to read this word: moron.

The "rest period" of Tabata is the greatest misnomer in the history of modern language. You're not resting but simply trying to determine whether the next interval may wind up being the last thing you accomplish in this lifetime. Also, when using an elliptical, it takes about five seconds to bring the pedals to a complete standstill, so it's not even a full rest period. I did eventually make it through all eight sets of the workout and, although some would prefer going on a 20-mile run uphill into the wind through snow naked and blindfolded rather than doing Tabata a second time, I have indeed incorporated it into my training routine.

Tabata's maximum effort doesn't always mean having to warn the people on the machines next to me that there's a high probability I may pass out on top of them. It doesn't have to be torture, just difficult. Rest assured that Tabata doesn't have to be your last words à la Kane's "Rosebud."

I've now done Tabata sprinting on grass, with a rowing machine, on a treadmill, and on a stair climber (anything that gets the heart rate up quickly). The bottom line is that no matter which method, it's all the same.

Get ready to suck air!

PART
II

Who's Running With Me?

Alone in a Crowd vs. Company While Going Solo

CHAPTER 5

Solitary Refinement

So long solo long!

It is difficult to correlate the title of Alan Sillitoe's famous short story, "The Loneliness of the Long Distance Runner," with today's plethora of running groups and mega-size marathons. The latter of which can find you running alongside 40,000 or more of your closest strangers and the entire racecourse filled with cheering spectators and entertainment such as mariachi bands and samba music provided every 34 yards. Isolation is not exactly the word that springs to mind.

For the vast majority of my running career since college, I relished the solitary nature of running. Henry David Thoreau said, "I never found the companion that was so companionable as solitude." Although that sounds a bit like someone welcoming a long stint in solitary confinement, I understood his thought. When I'm talking with myself on a run, well, at least I know somebody is listening. If the time comes that I mutter, "What'd you say?"—well, I guess I'd conclude it'd be a good idea to obtain running companions other than Mr. Solitude.

Certainly, I did run with others now and then. And I recall that when I lived in Boulder, Colorado, and crossed paths with legendary Frank Shorter while heading down the same trail that he casually invited me along. When he said, "Hi, I'm Frank," I had to concentrate very hard on recalling my name to respond in kind for what seemed like forever. I did settle in from there and we had a good conversation on our run together. He never alluded to his identity as a running star, and, although I lacked a pen for his autograph, I stopped just short of asking him to instead simply sweat on my singlet (never to be washed again).

Running was always a personal event to me, a disciplined activity done on my schedule, over my hills and my intervals, and on my own terms in going fast or slow depending on how I felt. As Frank Sinatra sang, I also wanted to fail or succeed at races based on training having been done *My Way*:

And now, the end is near,
And so I face the finish line.
My friends, I'll say it clear
The success of my time is all mine.

I've trained all by myself
I've run alone each and every day.
I know one thing for sure
I did it my way.

Yes, there were times, I finished slow
Tried going faster than I should go
But through the race, when things got rough
I plowed ahead and I was tough.
I hit the wall, but I stood tall
And did it my way.

Each solitary mile,
Every morning without delay.
I knew one thing for sure
I did it my way.

For what does a runner really have
If not himself, then he has not
To train the way he really wants
And not the pace of one who jaunts
Tough runs show, that I took the blows
And did it my way.

Okay, perhaps Mr. Sinatra had a little more success in his singing career than I did in my running career, but you get my drift. However, a few things eventually happened that led me in the direction of breaking from my solo runs and periodically going with others. First, I signed up to do a 50-mile run and, well, at some point during the latter stages of my 35- to 40-mile training runs I'd deplete my brain of coherent things to think about. I knew it might be time to look for running partners when I started asking myself, "Did you hear the one about . . . ?" I usually had.

So to avoid repeating jokes to myself, I joined some guys on Saturday mornings to occupy the middle miles of my extra long runs. I was the youngest and, at times, we were on slightly different planes of conversation. They were inclined to discuss things like new minivans and 401(k) plans. I was years away from a baby crib, let alone a minivan, and my 401(k) had less money than their kids' piggy banks.

I did enjoy their company but eventually the 50-mile race came and went and other commitments got in the way of group runs on Saturday mornings. I continued with my solitary running and subsequently we moved. In our new neighborhood I consistently crossed paths during my runs with four other solitary runners. We ultimately banded together and began meeting in the early mornings a few times a week. We had different backgrounds, careers, political leanings, and so on, but we also shared a common bond of willingness to head out in the dark of winter at 5:30 a.m. on icy roads with howling winds and a below-zero wind chill. United in our being NUTS!

Sure, we had to initially sort through the male territorial markings of pushing the pace, although afterward, we were always convinced it was another one of us who was more dramatically picking up the speed. We learned which political

> I knew it might be time to look for running partners when I started asking myself, "Did you hear the one about . . . ?" I usually had.

topics were best to avoid after glycogen depletion set in, and we had the implicit ability to ignore the natural cacophony of each other's spontaneous bodily sounds. We tolerated each other's quirks, including one of us running in shorts in 20-degree weather, while I almost incurred frostbite from just looking at him.

We had the rhythmic early-morning routine of the neighborhood down pat, knowing exactly where and when we'd see the woman running with her dog as well as the runner who, despite encountering us countless times, could never respond with a "Hi," let alone a wave or even a nod of the head. This was despite our most obnoxious efforts to coax something out, including a very off-key barbershop quartetlike good morning serenade.

> We learned which political topics were best to avoid after glycogen depletion set in, and we had the implicit ability to ignore the natural cacophony of each other's spontaneous bodily sounds.

Our claim to fame was once having the professional runners from the Hansons-Brooks Distance Project come down the road behind us and being able to stay ahead of them until they eventually turned down a side street. Admittedly, they were on a slow run while we were sprinting as though being chased by a crazed, hungry grizzly bear. Hey, whatever pumps up our aging egos.

We also witnessed the personality morphing of one mild-mannered member of the group. The one who instantly became a maniacal Hulk Hogan–like character when a van came a wee bit too close to us one morning and he aggressively challenged the driver to a smackdown. I'm still not sure whether the van's suddenly close proximity or his instantaneous personality change was more frightening.

I underwent solitary refinement over the years as I migrated away from solo running every day and learned the benefits of running with others. However, there also seems to be a point of compromise between running alone and in a group. I've recently noticed two (and sometimes more) runners keeping each other company on the roads, but they have headphones on. They are clearly a running oxymoron of going *alone together*.

Running presents a few other oxymorons, including feeling like the *living dead* at a marathon gone badly or being *absolutely uncertain* when I'll return from an injury. There are also our efforts in calculating an *accurate estimate* of how far we ran.

And will I someday ditch solo running altogether and be a daily group runner? Well, the oxymoronic answer is a *definite maybe*.

Look at Me Now

Is it conceit to tweet your feats?

We've all heard that old philosophical question "If a tree falls in a forest and no one is around to hear it, does it make a sound?" I won't even try to answer this given the necessity of thereby addressing issues of unperceived existence, the unobserved world, and reality. My reality is that's all well beyond my capabilities for philosophical analysis. I don't go much deeper than pondering what if there were no hypothetical questions? Or what was the greatest thing before sliced bread?

On first hearing the forest question, I didn't get much past the mystery of how'd the entire tree actually fall over by itself. However, if one were to analogize this query to the sport of running, the question might be "If a runner sets a personal running record in the forest and no one else is there, did it really happen?" In our present era of ubiquitous social media, the answer is undeniably "Of course, you Twitterhead. Everyone would know within eight seconds!"

That's because today's runner is adept, as well as interested, in letting everyone know about his or her wonderful running accomplishments. Social media has not only provided terrific new verbs, including tweeting, blogging, texting, and podcasting, but it's also given runners the ability to quickly disseminate their results and race photos. I may be one of the remaining 14 people in North America without a personal Facebook page, but

I do recognize the benefits of certain elements of social media. However, I'm not the type who is compelled to let people know I finally cooked a soufflé without it sinking, let alone communicate my great training run or race result. If I were that runner in the woods, no one would know of the stellar running performance unless I advised a relatively uninterested chipmunk on the way back to my car.

Perhaps this all stems from my first marathon, which occurred when I was 17 years old. That race was much different from today's mega races. It had fewer than 100 runners, about eight spectators (if you include the two stupefied park maintenance staff wondering what in the name of insanity we were doing), a couple of meager aid stations, and no finisher medals or the other amenities so common today. The only people aware of my performance were the ones within earshot of the bellowing guy with the megaphone who announced the names and times of runners as they crossed the finish line. This was well before today's ability to track runners by their race chip and have not only finishing times automatically sent via cell phone texts but also various split times along the racecourse. Perhaps someday they'll have tracking ability so that someone following my progress might receive a more descriptive text saying, "Bottomed out at 21.3 miles. Going to be a death march from here on out. Have pity on him. It's not pretty."

Certainly I shared the result of my first marathon with my immediate family and a few close friends, but I didn't feel compelled to broadcast it beyond that point because the achievement was personal and internally savored. To me, some things happen on a need-to-know basis and not everyone needs to know. I'm the type of person who is as disinclined to put a bumper sticker on my car stating something to the effect that *My 3rd Grader Can Do Long Division* as I am in putting on a *Boston Marathon* sticker. (Of course, if I did put the former on, I'm sure I'd be upstaged by someone with a sticker saying *My 3rd Grader Built the Calculator to Allow Your 3rd Grader to Do Long Division.*)

I'd actually be more inclined to stick a poor result on my car and maybe get some words of encouragement or sound advice.

Maybe I can market humbling bumper stickers, maybe one displaying the first time I figuratively crashed and burned during a marathon. My goal of negative splits turned out to be more like negative pits. I had the mother of all bonks. Not far into the second half of that marathon, I felt like my legs were laden with lead, and hallucinations entertained me the remainder of the way. Perhaps a bumper sticker detailing my inconsistent half-marathon splits, saying 1:22+1:43=BONK! Or perhaps a decal paraphrasing Julius Caesar, "I came. I ran. I bonked."

I don't need pats on the back for a good performance as much as I could use some words of commiseration for a bad one. I know I'm in the small minority here and that most runners are interested in displaying their accomplishments not only in their family rooms but also on their shirts, car bumpers, tattoos, Facebook, and blogs. And I do truly get it. It's an accomplishment and goal that you achieved and you want others to know about. That's fine, and

> My goal of negative splits turned out to be more like negative pits. I had the mother of all bonks.

it's a personal choice. If you want to put on your car a *100K* sticker or a *Twenty-Six Point Freaking Two* sticker then it's all well and good. *Hey, Honk if You Ran a Marathon!*

As I see more and more bumper stickers available at race expos, I wonder where we draw the line regarding what types of running achievements should be publicized. How about *Grabbed a Drink at an Aid Station While Opening a Gel Packet With My Teeth and Didn't Get Anything on My Shirt!* Might not fit on an average-sized bumper.

Not that it will come to pass, but if the day arrives that I get the Pulitzer for nonfiction literature, well, maybe I'd let my mom get a *Mother of Pulitzer Award Winner* sticker for her car. For her.

But for running and me, maybe someday I'll get something publicizing that I'm part of this larger group of running nuts. Something only runners would understand.

Maybe, *Got Toenails?*

Forecast: Partly Cloudy, Good Chance of Pain

Follow Sparky Anderson's words on your way to nirvana

Master Chief John Urgayle: *Pain is your friend, your ally, it will tell you when you are seriously injured, it will keep you awake and angry, and remind you to finish the job and get the hell home. But you know the best thing about pain?*

Lt. Jordan O'Neil: *Don't know!*

Master Chief Urgayle: *It lets you know you're not dead yet!*

   From the film G.I. Jane

Okay, admittedly not a movie classic, but classic lines to which runners can relate. I'm not going to debate whether runners pushing themselves to ludicrously ridiculous places of discomfort and pain is altogether a good or bad thing. But it's definitely a common thing.

As Russian novelist Fyodor Dostoevsky said, "Suffering is the sole origin of consciousness." Perhaps, with runners, it is fighting through the arrival of pain that makes us feel completely alive. Although, I'd definitely vote for the appearance of that often elusive euphoric feeling instead. A *runner's high* over a *runner's cry*.

There are legendary stories of elite runners going to tremendous depths of distress and pain. Champion runner Alberto Salazar was prematurely administered his last rites at the Falmouth Road Race finish line when his body temperature reached 107 degrees. A few years later, after he won the 1982 Boston Marathon, he was whisked to an emergency room for six liters of saline solution in an IV drip when his temperature dropped to 88. Apparently, a postrace temperature in the neighborhood of 98.6 was a bit elusive for Alberto.

Similar determination was seen at the 1996 U.S. Olympic Marathon Trials when eventual winner Bob Kempainen, cruising along at a 5:00-mile pace, became sick. Literally. Barely breaking stride, he bent over and tossed his cookies. (This occurred on national television, and in today's world of *Fear Factor*–like reality shows, this might be an engrossing—no pun intended—way to get viewers to actually watch a marathon race).

Kempainen kept going and it happened again as he briefly resembled a Weeble, wobbling yet never falling down, while also giving new meaning to the term Vomit Comet (what some call NASA's reduced-gravity training plane). Through stomach cramps and nausea, he threw up again and again. In the last three miles, Kempainen threw up six times and never relinquished his lead.

Strangely enough, the sicker he got, the faster he got. His last mile was under five minutes! Did the 1990s bring us not only grunge music and Beanie Babies but also *retch running* as a successful racing technique? Thankfully, the latter never really caught on.

After the race Kempainen said, "I'd be willing to do more than vomit to win this race." I'm not sure what other bodily functions he had in mind, but we got the picture (in more ways than one) of his tenacity. After the race, third-place finisher Keith Brantly aptly stated what many of us who watched and cringed were thinking: "This guy is the toughest human being on the face of the earth. I would have started crying and stopped."

Tom Courtney, the gold medal winner in the 800 meters at the 1956 Olympics, described the degree of pain he put himself through in that race: "It was a new kind of agony for me. I had never run myself into such a state. My head was exploding, my stomach ripping and even the tips of my fingers ached. The only thing I could think was, 'If I live, I will never run again.'"

Agony and distress are not reserved for the elite runners. Many of us have, in the midst of a difficult run, shared Courtney's sentiments. But we eventually dust ourselves off and jump back in the fray. If, as Master Chief Urgayle believed, pain is your friend, then at the end of a tough run, we'll have the company of an array of friends from Mr. Torment to Ms. Agony to Mr. Anguish.

We know exactly what we'll experience when we dive into the lactic acid pool and our carbohydrate fuel tank is well below empty. Armed with that potential, we partake anyway because we enjoy participating in things that make us feel more than vital. Sometimes we're the windshield and sometimes we're the bug, but either way, a full life is made up of these experiences, and

> Sometimes we're the windshield and sometimes we're the bug, but either way, a full life is made up of these experiences, and we must embrace the discomfort that may arise.

we must embrace the discomfort that may arise. As running philosopher Dr. George Sheehan said, "To keep from decaying, to be a winner, the athlete must accept pain—not only accept it, but look for it, live with it, learn not to fear it." This is a lesson learned through the experience of hard interval workouts, tempo-pace long runs, and of enduring races. We volunteer for these undertakings where the wheels may come off and nonrunners will question our collective wisdom. We may be NUTS! but also more crazy like a fox in wicking running socks.

No less a philosopher was Sparky Anderson, the Hall of Fame baseball manager of the World Series champions Cincinnati Reds and Detroit Tigers, who succinctly said, "Pain don't hurt." Sometimes it is mind over matter, and, as Mark Twain declared, "If you don't mind, it doesn't matter."

We runners will continue to plow forward, and maybe we're just a bit more comfortable at being uncomfortable. Many times in my running career I have questioned my maniacal approach to working through pain and my common sense IQ dipping well below feebleminded. From running with a stress fracture to keeping a daily running streak alive despite battling bronchitis, I have run beyond complete exhaustion countless times and did not hit just one wall but was bonked by a series of walls, feeling as though someone were adding weights to my back with each step. There was also the time I overexerted during an elliptical workout to the point of being about one pedal revolution from passing out. Otherwise known, in more basic layman terms, as "Hey, pea brain with the ashen face, tone the intensity down a notch or two!" Not exactly the behavior that's going to get the Mensa society knocking at my door. Perhaps the Dense-A society instead.

Singer Tom Petty didn't have running in mind per se when writing the lyrics to the song "Big

> **Running keeps us from rusting and makes us feel vibrant, challenges us, and pushes us to places we wouldn't otherwise have encountered.**

Weekend." But Petty encapsulates the sentiment of many runners quite nicely. Petty wrote, "If you don't run, you rust." And, yes, we even welcome the pain when it comes to visit. Bring it on and we'll make Master Chief Urgayle proud! As author T.S. Eliot said, "Only those who will risk going too far can possibly find out how far they can go."

There's an old saying "No pain, no gain." My version of that is more inclusive of running itself and the vitality and exhilaration it brings to our lives.

Namely, "No pain, how mundane."

CHAPTER 8

Every Dog Has Its Way

You can lead a dog, but you can't always make him a canine convert

As a runner, when I became a prospective parent, I dreamt of raising the next Steve Prefontaine or Joan Benoit Samuelson, and visions of running endless miles with my child danced in my head. Prospective Parent was not to be confused with Perspective Parent, the latter of which I had none.

Like some modern-day running Svengali, I was certain that no matter the predilections of my children, they would be lacing up their running shoes before knowing their ABCs. I envisioned the joy of having constant running companions just down my upstairs hallway. My children and I would eventually enter races together, enjoy cool-downs on our street, and bask in the black toenails we had in common.

My visions soon met my reality. Despite enthusiastically introducing my children to the wonders of running, it became quite clear that they were going to have their own interests and their own desires. The nerve of the little tykes!

Years down the line, I had one convert after my younger son realized that 120 pounds of desire wasn't enough to extend the football career of a running back beyond his middle school days. Unfortunately, as much as he loved dear old dad, my lone runner offspring preferred putting in the miles with his cross country teammates than with me. Go figure.

When my last child, and only daughter, had arrived (otherwise known in my eyes as the next Paula Radcliffe), I pulled out all the stops. I went so far as to form a local youth running team and serve as head coach. I didn't stop there. I also began a recess running program at her elementary school. My obsession to lure her into the world of running knew no boundary because she was my last great hope to discover the joy of fartlek.

My daughter humored me for a while, but before fifth grade and season two of the running team began, she delicately informed me she no longer wanted to participate with the team. After my wife finished administering CPR to me, I did compose myself, fought back tears, and asked, "Didn't you like your teammates?"

She said, "Sure, they were great. Lots of good times."

"Well, didn't you love the scavenger hunt candy runs?"

"Yeah, dad. Those were fun and tasty."

"How about the team T-shirts, the water balloon relay races, the trophies, the ribbons, the mashed potato mile run on Thanksgiving morning?"

"All good, Dad."

"Well clue me in, then, Sunshine. What is it you didn't like?"

She paused and looked me squarely in the eyes. It was a look I recall from many years ago when my first girlfriend was breaking it off. My daughter succinctly said, "Dad, well, it's the running part."

Ah, minor technicality, I thought. We can work through that little glitch. Subsequently, rational thinking eventually got the better of me, and I concluded that you can lead a daughter to the scenic cross country course, but you can't make her run.

I watched her gravitate into the world of competitive dancing and was resigned to the fact that running races with my kids was not in my immediate future. Truth was, it didn't appear to be in my distant future either.

My three children joined my wife in the ever increasing number of people in my home who weren't going to run with me. But I did not give up all hope. Where there's a will, there's a way. In my case it was "If there's a dog, I'll get my way." It was now time for a canine running companion.

My three children joined my wife in the ever increasing number of people in my home who weren't going to run with me. But I did not give up all hope.

Being a family without a pet, the sight of runners cruising along with their dogs never really registered much with me. But having promised our daughter a dog when her brothers went off to college, the dawn of pooch pacing was upon us when we purchased a dog at the local animal shelter. I had had my running dogma for years, and now I had my running dog. Or so I thought.

Henry the mutt joined our brood and I began reading about creating a canine training partner. I stopped short of organizing a running team for dogs in the neighborhood, but I did consult friends with running dogs and educated myself on how best to introduce running to him, what age to start, how far, how fast, and so on.

The problem was I had a preconceived notion that all dogs love to run. I don't mean run to get the tennis ball across the back yard or chase the squirrel up the tree. I mean run as in nudging my pajama bottoms at 5:00 a.m. with his leash in his mouth in the effort to get me out of bed because he was so excited to hit the roads. I imagined him constantly wagging his tail as we bounded across miles of trails together while he obeyed my every command. I'd read about the dogs that would go many, many miles at a stretch with no complaints. That's what they do, I thought. I'd seen the Iditarod where dogs travel over 1,000 miles in less than two weeks via mushing. My dog? Not so *mush*.

Let's just say it was a good month if I could get him to run a total of two miles in four weeks. If he were a greyhound, he'd break tradition and might only run if the rabbit began chasing him. Perhaps my daughter had been talking to him, but the fact was he simply did not revel in the joy of running. But I was persistent given that a dog has to exercise, and I didn't really picture him riding a bicycle or using a stair climber.

> I'd seen the Iditarod where dogs travel over 1,000 miles in less than two weeks via mushing. My dog? Not so *mush*.

When we first began I'd return from my daily run and grab his leash and would then very slowly introduce to him running. We would start off at a snail's pace, but it became quite clear he preferred the pace of an elderly mollusk and the latter even seemed a bit too fast for his liking.

I would oblige my new running partner, and we'd continue with an even slower saunter. One of the main problems that arose was he was compelled to at least try to urinate every six yards despite the fact that his bladder had been empty for the past quarter mile. I've had plenty of running partners who from time to time needed to stop to readjust their clothing, take a quick potty break, open a gel packet, take a water break, or even toss their cookies. But those pit stops would be relatively short and usually occurred no more than once during a run. He required more pit stops, or more aptly piss stops, than an amateur jalopy driver at the Indianapolis 500 and ultimately left me pissed.

It wasn't just the frequency of his urinary demands or his need to sniff every passing flower, tree, or bush that did us in. It was also the fact that his stopping came with no premonitory warning let alone a pee-monitory warning. Like any good running partner should, he offered no words of warning of an impending stop like, "Hey, going to come to a quick standstill at that lilac bush up the road."

Instead, we'd have entered a stretch where I was thinking that perhaps he was finally getting the hang of running together and then BAMMO my arm with the leash was suddenly yanked from my shoulder socket as he came to a screeching halt. He had the uniquely chameleon ability to transform from adorable canine into anchors aweigh, and away I'd go.

I finally gave up and concluded he shared something with the other nonrunners in the home. For now he'd get his exercise through long walks and sprinting around the dog park. Despite my pointing out to him the various dog runners and their owners traversing our neighborhood, he remained unwavering in his aversion for long-distance running.

I show him the *Homeward Bound* movie from time to time in the hope he'll recognize that animals do run long distances. I still cling to the whimsical dream he'll be my running partner when I give it another shot with him.

If not, my daughter better dust off her running shoes because I'm coming her way.

Epilogue

In the interest of not libeling a canine, I did give it one more shot with Henry. About six months after this chapter was written something miraculous occurred. Quite surprisingly, he became a plodder, a trotter, and then a true running dog. I asked no questions (not that he'd be forthcoming with answers) as to what finally inspired him. Truth be told, he had his stipulations such as only trails, no leash (where allowed), and a postrun biscuit. Not overly demanding and settled with a paw handshake, I happily welcomed having a housemate willing to run with me anyplace, anytime, anywhere. And if he could smile, I know he would. I am.

PART

III

Lacing 'Em Up and Laying 'Em Down

Wins, Losses, and a Whole Lot in Between

CHAPTER 9

What Are the Odds That Older and Slower Equal Better?

Using your shortcomings to your advantage in the long run

After my first semester of law school, all the grades, based on exams, for five classes were simultaneously posted. I was standing next to my friend as we perused the list when he suddenly let out an audible sigh on seeing that, despite his efforts, he'd failed four of his classes and obtained a C in Contracts. With tongue firmly planted in cheek, he jokingly said, "That'll teach me for spending too much time studying Contracts."

My friend's talents didn't translate to law school, and he was astute enough to realize this; he withdrew and became successful in business. But had he truly done as poorly as his grades indicated? Or had he overachieved a bit given that his natural abilities were aligned with business and not at all with law? Has the person with an IQ of 140, who gets a 97 on the exam, performed better than the 109 IQ guy who achieved an 89?

We all have our particular skills, but as applied to running, perhaps our body type or our preponderance of fast-twitch muscle fibers over slow twitch makes us less suited for endurance events than to other athletic activities. But those factors aren't taken into account. The winner of a race is normally determined to be the one who gets from point A to point B before anyone else (and doesn't take the subway à la Rosie Ruiz). Simple, basic, and fair. But is it? Is it possible that the best performance on race day came from the 36-year-old female middle-of-the-pack runner with an endomorphic body type, flat feet, and a genetically average V̇O2max and with a limited sleep schedule because of a teething baby at home? Maybe.

The best performance would be uncovered if we began leveling the playing field by handicapping races and giving runners certain advantages or compensations to equalize their chances of being the winner. Other sports allow players of different proficiencies to play against each other on somewhat equal terms through golf handicaps (calculating a net score from the number of strokes actually played) and chess handicapping (extra moves or removing pieces) as well as bowling (adding to one's score). Age-graded calculators allow older runners to handicap their performance and compare their time to what they'd have run in their prime, and some races compensate for a runner's weight by providing divisions for males in the Clydesdale category (around 200 pounds) and for women in the Filly (also labeled Athena and around 150 pounds) class. Some races handicap things further and use age-weight-gender calculators to grade performances and determine the best performance on race day. But we don't need to stop there. Handicapped horse races require each horse to carry specified weights in saddle pads to equalize the chances of the competitors. Maybe we should start having the elite runners wear weighted vests to level the playing field or more specifically the racecourse. Wouldn't it be great to see a retired 61-year-old schoolteacher and grandmother of five from Poughkeepsie, New York racing the winner of the 2011 Boston and New York City marathons, Geoffrey Mutai (weighted vest and all), to the finish line for first place? The Graceful Kenyan versus the Gray-Haired Grandma!

Race directors aren't inclined to determine race results by factoring in whether you're coming back from an injury or competing with a significant head cold or you celebrated your job promotion into the early morning the night before. But I'm now fighting for Average Ricky or Roxie Runner in stating that we need to move beyond the simple handicap factors of age, sex, and weight in calculating the best performance.

Let's start with the basics and plug in miles per week of training and speed work. Heck, if you're running 140 miles a week and doing solid interval training, then you should be running elite times! Big whoopee for your sub-2:05 marathon time, Mr. Lean Gene with the high calf muscles, slim legs, smooth stride, and high-altitude hometown! Running fast is your job! What about the stocky 43-year-old 3:24 marathon guy with tree trunk thighs squeezing in 40 miles a week between working two physically demanding jobs, coaching his children's soccer teams, and doing limited speed work because of Achilles tendinitis and a weak bladder requiring him to take two pit stops during a marathon? Try that one on, Mr. Speedy East African Star!

What the heck, let's also toss into the calculator whether you race better in the heat or cold, whether you're more suited for steep hills and long downhill stretches or a flat course, whether you are a natural forefoot striker, and whether you tapered for the race. Is your job (or nonrunning life) sedentary or physically active? Did you have the time to do a full prerace warm-up? Because I run better with a solid warm-up in the heat on a hilly course, then maybe my actual best performance was a good race time on a fairly frigid day on a pancake-flat course where I arrived late and had no warm-up time. Go figure.

So if you find a summer race that calculates handicaps including whether you have hay fever or not, how many extra miles per week you put on your legs by walking your dog daily, whether you average less than five and half hours of sleep per night, and whether you have a lower-than-normal hemoglobin count and that you never run negative splits and have a below-average sit-and-reach flexibility test score, well please let me know as soon as possible. That race has my name written all over it.

Similarly, I can just imagine if they'd also leveled the playing field in law school. If only final grades had factored in unproductive hours spent watching Big East college basketball, an attention span of under four seconds, and the number of weekend races run versus working on course study outlines.

I'd have been a clear shoo-in for valedictorian!

Count Me In on Counting Me Out

Other challenges after erasing 100-mile races from your bucket list

The concept of a bucket list has become popular recently. The idea being to create a list of experiences that one wants to accomplish before kicking the proverbial bucket. A bucket list may contain items like traveling to the Pyramids of Giza or adventurous activities such as swimming with dolphins or bungee jumping. Some people may list personal items such as rebuilding a relationship or more cerebral achievements like reading James Joyce's *Ulysses*. Of course, less scholarly minded people like me may also include things such as rolling down a steep hill while fully encased in bubble wrap.

Running a marathon is included on many people's bucket list, which in turn has generated debate amongst runners. Some view it as trivializing the accomplishment when it's a one-time deal and something to simply cross off a list. I don't have a problem with it because the more runners (even temporarily) the better, and most likely some bucket list marathoners get hooked on running and stick with it even after crossing it off their list. If my list includes learning how to ride a mechanical bull, would other bull riders frown at me if I crossed it off my list once I mastered an electric bucking bronco? Heck, they'd probably be happy that the line for the next ride would be shorter.

Many runners may not have a formal bucket list but have running-related goals such as getting a Boston qualifier or achieving a guaranteed entry time for the New York City Marathon. Others may have a list of races they want to participate in such as the Hood to Coast Relay, the Comrades Marathon, or the Dipsea Race. I confess that in my earlier years I had some particularly challenging races on my informal list, which I've yet to accomplish, including the Pikes Peak Marathon and the Western States Endurance Run. I've now relegated these to a "Fuggedaboutit List," also known as an "It Ain't Gonna Happen List." I still have a list of extreme endurance challenges, but at some point I had to conclude that finishing the Leadville Trail 100 Run or the Marathon des Sables is about as likely to occur as my permanently switching to decaf or choosing to watch the complete boxed set of *The Best of Jerry Springer*.

As long as I'm able, I'll continue to challenge myself with the endurance of a marathon or the speed of a solid 10K, but I've now begun penning items on my running bucket list that are less conventional. I recall the words of my middle school track coach who, on the first day of sixth-grade practice, introduced the concept of running and racing on an oval track. His instructions were "Get moving, keep taking a left, and arrive back here as fast as you possibly can." Some races aren't designed with that simplicity. Many more are outlandish, challenging, and zany, including racing attached by a rope to a burro or, for those so inclined, to shed all inhibitions with the Dare to Go Bare race. There's also the Handcuffed Couples race in Buffalo, New York, and lengthy looped courses where you collect a playing card each time you go around and compete for the best poker hand and the fastest race time. Some of the entrants on my bucket list of outlandish and challenging races include:

Krispy Kreme Challenge (Raleigh, North Carolina)

Here you'll hit the wall, not from glycogen depletion but from glycogen overload. The race consists of running two miles and then consuming a dozen donuts. Once that gastronomic challenge is completed, don't lean against the wall while undergoing a hallucinatory sugar high. Instead, race the two miles back with a hefty anchor of fried dough residing in your stomach. The only race where you'll weigh more at the finish line than you did at the starting line.

Living History Farms Race (Urbandale, Iowa)

With seven crossings of a knee-deep creek and terrain that includes mud that's thick enough to keep you wondering whether your shoes and ankles will be dislodged, this seven-mile cross country race is uniquely challenging and competitive. Not only will you navigate over hay bales and fallen trees and around horse manure and blowing cornstalks, you'll also dodge farm animals and crawl to the tops of slick gullies. Need I say more?

Naked Pumpkin Run (various locations)

The naked part doesn't refer to the pumpkin itself, but, rather, this is a run in which race attire is optional. Enjoy the anonymity of running with your favorite carved gourdlike squash on your head and nothing else on but your running shoes.

Ultimate Runner Race (Winston-Salem, North Carolina)

Like a runners' pentathlon, this uniquely challenging multi-event includes (during the course of an evening) racing a mile, a 400-meter race, an 800-meter race, a 100-meter dash, and a 5K cross country race. Not for the meek of heart or the weak of speed.

If you see me someday at the Empire State Building Run-Up or dressed like a giant ape at the Denver Gorilla Run, rest assured, furry costume or not, I'm still trying to run as fast as possible. It's just that recovery time is a little shorter than, say, the Self-Transcendence 3100 Mile Race in Queens, New York, that, years back, had briefly made my race bucket list during an impetuous moment. With the unique races, I also get the opportunity for new personal records. It's a one-time deal to run a race like the Bisbee 1000 in Arizona where you run 4.2 miles at mile-high altitude with more than 1,000 stairsteps included. You can also participate in the Ice Man Competition of the event and race up a set of 155 stairs while holding a 10-pound block of ice in a set of antique metal tongs. I can't say I've got an established PR going into that particular race. And if I can find a race in Auckland, New Zealand, where I can run while displaying my newly acquired talents of juggling bowling pins and yodeling, well, I can knock three things off my bucket list in one fell swoop!

CHAPTER 11

Refraining From Explaining

A poor performance may be unjust, but needs no justification

There's often a consistent theme when participants discuss a performance in which the results were not what they would have hoped for. Many people initially own up to their unduly disappointing performance by saying, "No excuses." However, that prefatory comment is often followed by the old qualifying conjunction of "but." As in the rather feeble "I really have no excuses for not running better, but I have been fighting pneumonia the last few days, I forgot to taper, the dew point was too high, and I think I pulled my adductor magnus or perhaps my peroneus longus. Also, they only had rigatoni at the pasta bar last night, and I only run well with angel hair. Plus it was above 64.7 degrees Fahrenheit, and that's my Achilles' heel. And the sport drink at the aid stations was lemon-lime and I'm more of a fruit punch guy. But again, like I said, no excuses."

Sports bring a high level of creativity to athletes in explaining their performances. Runners are no exception, and that includes elite runners. Khalid Khannouchi was a great runner and holds the American marathon record. However, when he dropped out of the marathon at the World Championships years back, his excuse for his poor performance was that he'd developed blisters because of the slow pace (irrespective of the fact that he could control the pace), requiring him to take more steps. His then wife and coach Sandra said, "He doesn't know how to run slow. When he runs slow, he gets tired." Khalid added, "My legs just got too heavy because of the slow pace." So let me get this straight. The slower he goes, the more tired he becomes? Kind of like a reverse tempo run. And it must therefore follow that he doesn't tire as easily the faster he goes? Hmmm. Perhaps that's the genetic makeup it takes to run a 2:05 marathon like Khalid has done, although it's kind of like saying "I would have done a lot better on that exam if it hadn't been so simple." I never had that problem; the more elementary the better. Test me with Is a 10K longer than a 5K? How many letters in bonk? Provide a word that rhymes with "pace" and feel free to use "race." What city does the Boston Marathon finish in? I'm good with that quiz. Don't even need the curve.

It's obviously not just the elites who feel compelled to offer excuses. I've heard (and offered) many explanations for poor race performances. There's the prevalent yet flawed justification of "I was just using the race as a training run." Rigghhtt! You just paid a $50 entry fee, drove 90 minutes on a Saturday morning to the race, internally debated for hours about your prerace snack, broke out your lucky singlet and new race shorts, and made sure you were in the first row of runners at the starting line, all to run a training run in a torrential downpour? Yeah, sure. Anyone who believes that, well, I'll sell you my new training program on how to run a three-hour marathon on 17 miles per week and a diet of donuts, hot dogs, soda, and fries.

There's an almost endless stream of excuses proffered by runners, such as I went out too fast, I went out too slow, my shoelaces were too tight, I overtrained, I undertrained, I had to go to the bathroom, I chafed, I blistered, I had a stomach ache, the mile markers were off, and so on. But why do we offer excuses? When you get right down to it, who cares? Our coworkers and nonrunning friends wouldn't really know a horrible performance from a heroic performance, and our running friends have all had their share of bad races, so they understand a tough day on the roads. And what do you care since you know that any excuse you provide is far from the truth. Oh sure, there are plenty of us, me included, who push it as hard as we can for the best time possible on that given day. But that's just it. The bottom line is to give it your max effort, and if your time or place is not what you hoped, then it's simply the fact that some days you hit the wall and some days you get the pleasure of being escorted around it.

There's also a growing category of runner for whom some of us could take a lesson. Race results aren't significant enough to them to even bother with manufacturing excuses. They run more for the pure enjoyment of the activity and to finish and couldn't care less if they just achieved their fastest race time or were completely depleted of energy at the end. They aren't dialed into the creed of former marathon world record holder Steve Jones who said, "If I am still standing at the end of the race, hit me with a board and knock me down, because that means I didn't run hard enough." Mr. Jones' approach is not exactly high in their list of motivating quotations.

The joy, for this type of runner, of simply partaking over an emphasis on wins and losses and personal best versus personal worst times, reminds me of when my 6-year-old son first became involved in youth sports. The focus was, similar to that of many runners these days, on participation over competition. This was no longer Vince Lombardi's Little League, rooted in his credo that winning was the only thing. The new slogan was more "Winning isn't everything. It's not even anything." No winners. No losers. No score. This wasn't the old Knute Rockne line of "Win one for the Gipper," but more "Just go and play, you little nippers."

The fact is as I became older, I jumped the proverbial shark. Or in the case of my running times getting slower, the clock jumped me. When you're physically incapable of matching your best results from years past, you can either hang up the shoes or choose to define success in other ways. Legendary UCLA basketball coach John Wooden said it best, "Do not let what you cannot do interfere with what you can do."

Oh, I still have my finishing time as a focus. But I'm satisfied if, on that day, I've given my max effort, that Steve Jones would be proud of my energy depletion at the finish line. We can all enjoy the journey, without excuses, whichever way we choose. Hey, one runner's torment is another runner's thrill.

Who needs excuses when accepting reality works just fine?

Log Me In

Do elite runners put on their shorts one leg at a time?

A few years ago I learned that some of the training logs of all-time great marathoner Bill Rodgers (from the early- to mid-1970s) had been posted online. To me, this was way more exciting than the anticipatory hype Geraldo Rivera generated for his highly watched television special "The Mystery of Al Capone's Vault." But unlike Geraldo and his 30 million viewers, I wasn't going to be disappointed in the outcome. No sir, I foresaw that the logs would reveal Rodgers' training strategies, his primary workouts that pushed him to greatness, and the intricate thought process of one of the most accomplished marathoners of all time. A greater treasure than Geraldo's ignominious unveiling of some old dirt and a few empty gin bottles in Al's vault.

Rodgers was a guy who, after his college career, stopped running completely and developed a two-pack-a-day cigarette habit, hung out at bars, and began running again while he was still smoking (not that he actually ran with a cigarette in his mouth). Perhaps this wasn't your classic path to greatness. Also, his return to racing occurred before the advent of comfy and efficient running clothing, and Rodgers began his road racing career attired in blue jeans or khakis (while churning out paces below five minutes per mile). Yet he subsequently went on to become a four-time Boston Marathon winner and a four-time

New York City Marathon winner. Surely he had some running secrets to reveal, if not some fashion suggestions.

However, once I began reading Rodgers' log I couldn't help but think of author F. Scott Fitzgerald's purported line that "The rich are different than you and me." Ernest Hemingway was said to have retorted, "Yes, they have more money." Similarly, the elite runners are indeed different than you and me. They run more. Go figure. Mystery solved.

The truth was Rodgers' entries established that he really was just an everyday Joe, although a Joe who often ran 130 to 155 miles per week. His logs contained rather mundane information, such as the weather, how his legs felt, distance covered, and, very rarely, his average pace. Rodgers was a bit like us to a degree. He had his lazy days where he didn't run, he called himself out for eating like a glutton (confirming the calories in versus calories out premise; he could gain weight even running mega-mega mileage), and he wasn't fond of running in frigid temperatures. His logs revealed that an elite runner is not immune to chafing or running poorly with a lack of adequate sleep. Imagine that. Not too terribly illuminating, but given that it was a glimpse inside, I remained riveted to every entry. I also learned he was quite normal in experiencing motivation issues from time to time and was fond of the simplicity of describing his pace as *easy, okay, good,* or *slow*. Of course, I can quickly extrapolate that his okay pace was likely tantamount to my version of phenomenal pace.

Compared with modern running logs, Rodgers' entries were minimalist. Today we have information overload because we can input copious data through online logs. This includes entries for calories per day, resting heart rate, hours of sleep, training heart rates, cross-training activities, course elevation, fluid intake, weight training, and so on. A bit more than I care to know, even if it's about myself. I imagine logs will soon emerge with the opportunity to indicate the number of spits and burps per run, heel strikes compared to midfoot strikes, significant ideas generated per hour, shoelace-length-to-eyelet ratio, and the degree of euphoria produced.

Admittedly, some logged information can be important for revealing certain training trends. Like when the painful alarm is about to sound on too many miles per week, when an injury is residing just around the corner, or when to back off the intensity of training if one's resting heart rate is on an upward trend. I am more Captain Basic, though. I diligently keep track of my miles per week and the pace of my speed workouts, but that's it. I'm not into examining things like bar graphs of my speed compared to degrees Fahrenheit to establish my optimal race temperature.

> I imagine logs will soon emerge with the opportunity to indicate the number of spits and burps per run, heel strikes compared to midfoot strikes, significant ideas generated per hour, shoelace-length-to-eyelet ratio, and the degree of euphoria produced.

I also recognize that a log may provide pertinent information about why a poor race performance transpired. However, the reality is if I implode during a marathon, it's usually not because I failed to put in enough miles or tapered insufficiently or lacked enough long tempo runs. No, the reason my time was relatively lousy is about as subtle as a flying brick. Such as going out at 15 seconds per mile under goal race pace for the first 10 miles, which indicates two things. First, I can be about as sharp as a marble on occasion. Second, I must have some odd subconscious attraction to the crushing feeling of a rather enormous elephant resting on my shoulders while I'm running. The joy of which inevitably greeted me when my self-induced, all-everything depletion set in.

I'm not sure we'd glean much insight into future athletic performances if we looked at the diaries of some of the great, yet unlikely, accomplishments in sports. For example, Michael Jordan's legendary status was enhanced by his play during game

5 of the NBA Playoffs in 1998 when he was quite ill. If Jordan's log were available, it would have read something to this effect of this:

> Woke up with extreme nausea, shaking and sweating profusely. No strength to even get out of bed. Feel paralyzed. Head spinning. Doc says food poisoning or stomach virus. Advised no way I'll play tomorrow. Stayed in bed until few hours before tip-off. Extremely weak, dizzy, almost passed out and came close to falling asleep on the bench, but I played almost the entire game. We won. I had 38 points, 7 rebounds, 5 assists, and 3 steals. Collapsed at end.

Despite his stellar performance, I doubt that before game 6, Jordan tried to replicate his condition from the previous game with his next entry reading, "I have to find more of that contaminated chicken parmesan!"

Or what about the log of Pittsburgh Pirates pitcher Doc Ellis who threw a no-hitter in 1970 under the influence of, for the lack of a better term, an acid trip. His log entry would have read something to the effect of this:

> Didn't know I was pitching today, let alone that we were playing a game. Perhaps not the best idea to have gotten high on LSD while in Los Angeles and before learning I would be pitching in San Diego later that evening. Got to game about 90 minutes before first pitch. Can't remember much about game. Sometimes couldn't see my catcher. Pitched a no-hitter. Go figure.

I doubt other pitchers, or Ellis for that matter, chose to follow that pregame pitching routine. Running also has produced outcomes where examining a log may not have been predictive of the result. For example, U.S. World Championship marathoner Nick Arciniaga engaged in extremely hard marathon training (130 to 150 miles per week) for the 2010 Chicago Marathon but ran a disappointing (to him) time of 2:18:12. His goal was sub-2:10. For the 2011 Houston Marathon, Arciniaga had not done his normal mega-mile marathon training because he was only serving as the pacesetter for his teammate Brett Goucher during the first 25K. But Arciniaga felt good at that juncture and kept right on going. And going. And going. He finished in second place with a personal record 2:11:30! Subsequently, after another solid marathon training buildup for the 2011 World Championships, Arciniaga finished a disappointing 41st (2:24:06). Sometimes the performances we're anticipating don't materialize, no matter what's written in the logs.

In the end though, examining logs is way more appealing than examining the empty gin bottles Geraldo uncovered in Capone's vault. The bottles may be indicative of an amazing prohibition party in the roaring 1920s, but there is nothing much more enjoyable than tallying up the miles in a solid week of running or logging in a PR performance.

Maybe things would have been different for Capone if, instead of running bootleg rackets, he had been an actual runner. He could have been logging miles instead of his many years at Alcatraz prison. Of course, that would have ultimately deprived us of the slang term for something that is overhyped and provides disappointing results: *Al Capone's Vault*.

If there were a TV show from the 1970s of *The Mystery of Bill Rodgers' Running Logs*, it would at least be captivating in the nuggets revealing that Bill was (and is) very much a regular guy. He is like you and me and does put on his shoes one foot at a time.

Back then, he just did it a lot more often, kept his shoes going longer distances, and, in the end, moved those shoes a heck of a lot faster.

Mystery solved.

PART

IV

The Road to Injury Is Paved With Foolish Intentions

Injuries Come and Go, But Stubbornness Remains

CHAPTER 13

Runner, Heal Thyself!

Self-diagnosis begins with a dim guinea pig for a patient

My fingers tapped feverishly like an out-of-control jackhammer on my thigh. Beads of sweat formed on my brow, and others in the waiting area exhibited similar looks of anxiety. I felt the same trepidation from years ago, brought on by my fourth-grade spelling bee. I longed for it to be the simple shame of a first-round exit, having forgotten the apparently key rule that every word has a vowel. But, no, this scenario had far greater repercussions.

Suddenly, a nurse said my name, so I bolted up and gingerly walked down the hallway to the man who held the fate of Western civilization in his hands.

Okay, perhaps a slight bit of hyperbole. However, to me, his impending proclamation regarding my ongoing knee pain would result in one of three critical outcomes. First, he could advise me that the daily activity I'd been addicted to since I was 11 years old (besides *Cap'n Crunch*) would have to be tossed aside like a well-worn pair of running shoes. Only to be inadequately replaced with a life sentence of satisfying my endorphin addiction with the sadistic elliptical machine. The latter producing depths of oxygen deprivation that left me feeling like I'd just reached the summit of Mount Kilimanjaro with an elephant in my backpack and one heartbeat away from needing immediate mouth-to-mouth resuscitation.

Second, he could provide hope that a cure was in sight. However, he'd also confirm my wife's viewpoint that I'm entirely deprived of even a smidgen of common sense regarding the treatment of an injury. Perhaps the definition of healed doesn't mean limping through a 10-mile run while wheeling along a push-controlled IV morphine drip. Maybe some exaggeration there on the morphine thing, but you get the depths of my inane behavior. Over the previous three months I'd ignored every cardinal rule of healing an injury. This was despite my possessing an abundance of knowledge on injury treatment. I'd haughtily concluded that it applied to all other runners but me.

Each morning I'd arise and engage in my new hobby of seeing how I could best prevent my injury from healing. As the third month of my running hiatus crept onward, I had to dig deep to come up with effective nonhealing ways. But never under estimate the depths of my injury idiocy. I was good at this!

RULE 1: *Listen to your body. Don't mask discomfort with pain relievers before attempting exercise.* Broke that one early on. It was so last month and so many ibuprofen capsules ago. Apparently pain should not be viewed as a nutritional deficiency only remedied with an increase in the intake of anti-inflammatory pills.

RULE 2: *Don't stretch a sprain; let it heal first.* Been there. Violated that.

RULE 3: *If you can't run without pain, you shouldn't be running.* I adhered to the mindless approach that says, if the agonizing pain is no worse than yesterday, go for a run.

You'd think I would quit while I was behind, but on it went. If I was supposed to be listening to my body, rest assured my volume control was on mute. I figured if I couldn't run 10 miles because of knee pain, walking the distance instead, with a distinct limp, wouldn't set me back. Brilliant. If experience is the name we give to our mistakes, I was the most experienced runner in North America. Just not the brightest, wick-drying neon shirt in the closet.

The final thing, after further testing, that the doctor could tell me was that surgery was the only solution. A very small part of me actually hoped I'd be able to utter words similar to Rocky Balboa's near the end of his first fight with Apollo Creed, "Cut me, Mick!" Not that having a tube-like viewing instrument rummaging around in my knee while under anesthesia ranked way up there on my bucket list. However, I was somewhat resigned to the fact that surgery might be a solution and the one approach I hadn't yet mastered on my home-treatment plan.

Each morning I'd arise and engage in my new hobby of seeing how best I could prevent my injury from healing. As the third month of my running hiatus crept onward, I really had to dig deep to come up with effective nonhealing ways.

But to get where I was, sitting on an examining table and awaiting my fate, we need to go back three months to the beginning of my ordeal. Back before a total of 280 icings of my right knee had transpired (such that just the mere opening of the freezer drops the temperature of my right lower leg by 11 degrees).

Back before I had embarked on an intensive knee anatomy course of study. Lesson one being that I didn't actually possess an anterior crucial ligament (which always seemed redundant to me because aren't all ligaments crucial?) Apparently, though, I did have an anterior cruciate ligament. Eventually I also knew my patellofemoral groove from my pes anserine bursa.

My newly acquired anatomical knowledge propelled me to spend seemingly endless hours on the Internet engaging in the addictive game of amateur orthopedic wiz and arriving at dozens of potential diagnoses for my knee pain. I suffered from my own form of OCD, otherwise known as obsessive–compulsive diagnosing.

I came up with everything from Lyme disease (don't burden me with the logic that because this was a winter injury there was virtually no likelihood of having been bitten by a tick) to osteo-chondritis dissecans (I just liked being able to say that one).

Attributing my ongoing pain to your run-of-the-mill knee sprain that I wasn't allowing to fully heal was way too easy. I departed from the belief of Leonardo da Vinci that *simplicity is the ultimate sophistication*. I adhered more to the notion that *complicated is the ultimate arrogance*.

My irrational search for a diagnosis found me more comfortable consulting with medically uneducated strangers in cyberspace than seeking the expert opinion of someone who may have actually read a medical textbook. Let alone one who had gone to medical school and five years of orthopedic residency training.

Rather than admit I had an injury severe enough to require seeing a physician, I was more content to consult with some mate in Australia who'd posted info on an obscure message board related to cross-country skiing about his knee symptoms, which closely resembled mine. Most importantly, the bloke had actually healed! I felt a glimmer of hope coming all the way from the land Down Under.

> I departed from the belief of Leonardo da Vinci that *simplicity is the ultimate sophistication.* I adhered more to the notion that *complicated is the ultimate arrogance.*

My absurd approach to belittling the significance of my injury reminded me of the movie line from *Monty Python and the Holy Grail*. That's where the Black Knight, after getting both his arms lopped off by King Arthur's sword, continues to try to battle on and illogically but dogmatically bellows, "It's just a flesh wound! I've had worse."

Every running injury I ever had was just a flesh wound. Ultimately though, my light bulb moment eventually arrived. A rational thought finally entered my head and offered, "After three months of pain being your constant walking companion, perhaps this is a bit more significant than a flesh wound?" Ya think?

My three-month odyssey had begun innocently enough when I felt a slight discomfort on the inside of my right knee while completing a run. Of course, as most runners know, it's not really an injury if the following occur:

1. One can walk after a run without dragging a leg and leading others to believe that you're practicing for a role as Igor in *Young Frankenstein.*

2. Anti-inflammatory pills can mask at least 84 percent of the pain and get you through the next day's run.

3. You can complete the first mile of a run without a series of contortionist moves (done to avoid placing weight on the affected area), which make you appear like the halftime performer who twists all body parts enough to get inside the miniature box.

My hesitation to see a specialist was based partly on a previous experience when I broke down and sought a medical opinion for a running malady. I'd had enough of playing the repetitive game of *Hammy Whammy*, where I'd pull a hamstring, let it heal, pull a hamstring, and so on. I was religiously stretching, weight training, getting massages, trying different forms of nutrition, refueling, running backward, doing yoga, pedaling backward on the elliptical, and using arnica, all to no avail. I was so busy trying to keep my hamstrings healthy, I barely had enough time to do what I actually wanted to do—run.

After explaining my situation in excruciating detail to a medical doctor with years of muscle and bone training in his repertoire, I waited with bated breath for words of wisdom and the magical cure for my chronic issue. He was my Yoda, my guru, and all-knowing one. "Tell me, Doc! Tell me the path to enlightenment!"

He looked at me with an expression of incredulity, and I wasn't sure whether it reflected his concern for my mental instability or my physical symptoms. He then uttered the words that became permanently seared in my memory bank. He said, "I really don't know. Perhaps it is MARS."

Momentarily digesting his alien diagnosis, I bellowed, "MARS? What in the name of Haile Gebrselassie is that? Is it fitness fatal? Help me, Doctor! Help me!"

He said, "Relax. It's my own acronym. It's *Middle-Aged Runner's Syndrome.*"

That was it. His illustrious opinion, based on years of experience, was that I was getting old, would become injured more, and would heal more slowly. "Well thank you, Dr. Obvious!" was all I could muster.

I did refrain from leaping off the examining table, grabbing him by his white-collared coat, and screaming, "That's it! That's all you got? You've arrived at the remarkable conclusion that I'm a runner who is no longer 20 years old! What gave me away? The receding hairline? Fallen arches? Crow's feet from running without sunglasses?"

I suddenly felt like one of those untied balloons that escape your grasp and whose evacuating air propels it wildly around the room before it plops limply on the ground. As I despondently exited the office, my air was effectively gone. (Apparently that was geriatric air according to someone in that examining room.)

But here I was again. Returning to the scene of the diagnosis. Okay, not the actual scene. I saw a different doctor this time but a similar examining table nonetheless. I was better prepared and provided him a single-spaced, one-page summary of my sequence of events over the previous 90 days. He read it, or at least he humored me and stared at the paper for a sufficient amount of time while perhaps instead dissecting the previous night's episode of *So You Think You Can Dance*.

He asked pertinent questions like "So exactly how long and how fast are you going on the elliptical, and do you have any sign of pain while doing that?"

I stammered a bit and embarrassingly avoided eye contact. Bless me, doctor, for I have sinned. I knew my answer depicting too far, too fast, too often, and too affirmative on the pain part was not going to generate an enthusiastic thumbs-up from him.

His illustrious opinion, based on years of experience, was that I was getting old, would become injured more, and would heal more slowly. "Well thank you, Dr. Obvious!" was all I could muster.

In the end, after a thorough exam and testing, the conclusion was that surgery wasn't a likely consequence. But an infusion of sanity to the masochistic elliptical routine and the overindulgent walking schedule would be in order to allow the significantly sprained ligaments in my knee to actually accomplish what they'd been trying to do despite my continuous undermining. Heal that is.

And heal they did. Albeit more tediously than the inch-by-inch shuffling pace after hitting the wall in a marathon. I promised that with any future injury, I would listen to that little physical therapist on my shoulder that says, "Be smart. Don't turn this minor injury into a lengthy ordeal. Patience is a virtue." Don't burden me with the fact that this was the same advice I'd ignored countless times after every injury over the last few decades.

I've officially removed the mute button on my listen-to-your-body volume control. The next time my illiotibial "band" starts playing a painful melody, I'm all ears.

And knees.

The Impact of Nonimpact

Finding true love with a sweat-inducing, quadriceps-exhausting machine

I always knew that my raison d'être, as far as physical activity was concerned, was running. Running was such an irreplaceable daily activity that during downtimes because of injury, my personality often morphed into a snarling, crazed wild animal that hadn't eaten in a week. Not real conducive to family harmony.

Over the years, when injury demanded it, I'd try my hand (or foot) at other forms of cardiovascular masochism but nothing could replace the joy of running. This was despite the evolution of numerous types of cross-training exercise machines that helped prevent an injured runner from turning into a giant puffy blob of adipose tissue caused by physical inactivity.

It was difficult to compare the running nirvana of effortlessly gliding along a lush woodchip trail in Oregon with the tedium of a joyless stair-climbing machine at the fitness club, surrounded by bright fluorescent lighting and piped-in elevator music. Not to mention that the bird's-eye view from the machine was often the large derriere of an out-of-shape guy in gray cotton sweatpants, sweating away on a treadmill in front of me.

For me, the operative word in cross-training is cross. As in I became cross when unable to run and had to resort to finding a comparable form of exercise. I tried everything at one time or another and appreciate the old adage that "One man's meat is another man's poison," or, in this case, "One injured runner's training mode is another runner's monotony."

> I tried everything at one time or another and appreciate the old adage that "One man's meat is another man's poison," or, in this case, "One injured runner's training mode is another runner's monotony."

I never quite found an adequate substitute. Biking didn't work because my piriformis muscle has a sitting shelf life of about 14 minutes. Thus, five-hour training rides leave me incapable, for days, of extracting myself from the bicycle seat. Pool running includes the mind-numbing repetition of running in water for an hour or more and gives me as much joy as counting grains of rice while blindfolded.

On it went. Finally, a few years ago as I was nursing a hamstring pull, I uncovered my personal panacea. Euphoria had arrived in the form of an enticing piece of machinery that mimicked the motion of running and provided an ecstatic endorphin rush. This exercise machine delivered a heart-pounding and high-intensity workout that left me still sweating long after a post workout shower, a drive back home from the fitness center, and breakfast. I spent the next few hours at work peppered with drops of forehead perspiration trickling onto my desk.

My newly discovered metallic friend, the enchanting elliptical, provided me unbridled enthusiasm. Gone would be the days of glancing at an exercise machine's display panel and sadly realizing that my workout to that point had been a whopping

46 seconds of excruciating tedium. No, this was vastly different, and I welcomed the display panel on the elliptical. Bring me your incline information, your calories burned, your revolutions-per-minute speed, your varied intensity levels, your heart rate info. I welcomed all of it. I was in low-impact heaven. My joints thanked me. My sweat glands thanked me. Most of all, I thanked me.

> Gone would be the days of glancing at an exercise machine's display panel and sadly realizing that my workout to that point had been a whopping 46 seconds of excruciating tedium.

No matter my injury, the elliptical would gently place me on its articulating foot pedals and off I'd go pain free and into the land of complete oxygen deprivation that I'd grown to love. The machine brought me to depths of complete and utter exhaustion that, strangely, I found breathtakingly captivating and addicting. Also, using the arm handles reacquainted me with upper-body muscles I hadn't visited with since my middle school football days. All cross-training hope was not lost.

Suddenly, the one who heretofore despised all forms of mechanical substitutions for running found himself completely obsessed with the elliptical. I couldn't help but hear Robert Palmer singing "Addicted to Love," although he was now singing "Addicted to Ellipticals":

> You're cruising fast, moving in place
> Quads and calves, they do ache
> Your heart pounds, your body shakes
> More time is what it takes.
>
> You can't rest, you can't stop
> There's no doubt, can't let go
> Lactate builds, legs are dead
> More time is all you need.

Whoa, you used to think you didn't like these machines, oh
yeah
It's closer to the truth to say you can't get enough
Gonna have to face it, you're addicted to ellipticals!

You see the display, flickering lights
You're grooving, with much fight
You heart beats, in double time
Another mile, and you'll be done, a one-track mind

You can't be saved
Maximum heart rate is what you crave
Churning legs, the motor hums
Perspiration, it amply comes

You used to think you didn't like these machines, oh yeah
It's closer to the truth to say you can't get enough
Gonna have to face it, you're addicted to ellipticals!

Yes, I miss the ability to run with my friends, but I have a knack
for being easily amused by ESPN SportsCenter for long periods
on the elliptical. I confess to actually enjoying, while on vacation
in Mexico, the weeklong use of a creaky elliptical in a darkly lit
basement gym while being entertained by ESPN Deportes with
no subtitles. All the while also having an enthusiastic Spanish-
speaking instructor lead an aerobics class right in front of me.
That experience clearly beats an elliptical workout in the fitness
center of a Washington, D.C., hotel, restricted to watching the
less-than-mesmerizing C-SPAN.

Along the way I've learned that one may find the results
regarding speed, distance, and so on to be different from brand
to brand of machine. One elliptical may indicate that your workout burned enough calories that you should now be down one
pant size and another will advise you that you've barely burned
off a cup of black coffee, a celery stick, and one Hershey's Kiss.

I recognize there are certain inherent drawbacks to elliptical
training. For example, no one will be waiting to put a medal
around your neck when you've beaten your personal record for

distance covered in an hour, and trying to give a high-five to the guy on the machine next to you may leave you hanging. Also, I haven't uncovered an elliptical race to enter, so my competitive juices are often fueled with occasional glances at the display panel of the physically fit guy pounding away a few machines over.

But like with any summer romance, the time would eventually come to return to school. Or, in this case, to road running again after my injury had healed. I did, though, remain loyal and did

One elliptical may indicate that your workout burned enough calories that you should now be down one pant size and another will advise you that you've barely burned off a cup of black coffee, a celery stick, and one Hershey's Kiss.

not cast aside my new love like an unsalvageable and overly worn-out pair of running shoes. I would not have to uncomfortably avert my gaze from the elliptical as I sauntered past it at the fitness club, while making my way over to the hamstring curl machine.

I interspersed elliptical training within my running regimen to provide my joints a dose of road respite. This also maintained my supply of dinner party conversation material of key SportsCenter viewing knowledge like knowing what NFL head coaches were on the hot seat six months before the season even began. Crucial stuff.

My new cross-training mantra is "Just take to the thighs on an ellipticaler's high."

CHAPTER 15

Behind Every Comeback Is a Foolhardy Failure

Fool me once, shame on me; fool me twice, runner rehab is in order

My heart was racing as I briskly walked to my car. The one-page typewritten paper remained tightly gripped in my hand, as I hadn't dared to glance at it just yet. Arriving at my car, I took a deep breath and tried to stop my quaking knees as I anxiously looked down for my results. This was the MRI report for my troublesome knee, which had prevented me from running a step for the longest stretch since I was in diapers at 14 months of age.

I had educated myself on every part of knee anatomy and was prepared to grasp the technical details from the radiologist's multiple-paragraph report. I hadn't gotten past the first sentence when a lump in my throat emerged and my heart sank. My body fell forward against my steering wheel. I was oblivious to the fact that I was leaning against my horn and serenading everyone in the parking structure.

After a stranger tapped on my window to shake me from my pity party, I reread the ominous words: "Deformity is noted in the central aspect of the posterior horn of the lateral meniscus, consistent with a meniscal tear."

A few months back I'd barely known a meniscus from a discus but now knew the menisci were two pads of cartilaginous tissue dispersing friction in the knee joint between the tibia and femur. They are attached to the fossae, or small depressions. This meant big depressions for me because a tear likely equaled a surgery.

I scanned through the remainder of the report, which was more benign, and I then began dialing my wife with the news. Suddenly though, in a rare lucid moment, the proverbial light bulb went off as I said out loud, "Wait a second here."

Despite knowing all the intricate medical terminology associated with my lower leg, this was tantamount to not seeing the forest for the trees. I'd failed to see the body for the knees.

To confirm my thoughts, I typed a word into my phone's dictionary app. Indeed, there it was! Miracle of miracles! Apparently, I might have known my knee's patellofemoral joint components, retinaculum, and articularis genu muscle, but I had failed to recognize something much more basic. Like position. I had to get my bearings.

Lateral referred to the outside of my knee! My pain only existed on my medial side, the inside of my knee, and the report revealed no *medial* abnormalities. Halleluiah! I went from the depths of despair to the throes of ecstasy in three short syllables.

I boldly dismissed the finding of a lateral meniscus tear and took comfort in knowing there was nothing of significance in the area of my knee pain. I was off to my scheduled appointment with my orthopedic doctor with a spring in my step, albeit still a limping spring.

> Despite knowing all the intricate medical terminology associated with my lower leg, this was tantamount to not seeing the forest for the trees. I'd failed to see the body for the knees.

I received confirmation from my doctor that the radiologist had overread the report, and I could resume running as soon as I was completely pain free. This was music to my ears and joy to my lower limbs. Admittedly, I'd never followed the simple advice of record-setting elite runner Jack Foster who said, "If it hurts, don't run on it." Brilliant words. My approach was, "If it hurts, run slower on it." Witless words.

> Admittedly, I'd never followed the simple advice of record-setting elite runner Jack Foster who said, "If it hurts, don't run on it." Brilliant words. My approach was, "If it hurts, run slower on it." Witless words.

All of which had, months back, caused my knee issue to go from mild to severe in one ill-advised mile too many. I left my doctor's office knowing that over my running career I'd had more comebacks than Rocky Balboa, Freddy Krueger, and Brett Favre combined. For me, it's not really an official comeback unless it follows my standard sequence:

1. Cause a significant overuse injury by illogically ignoring all signs of impending doom.
2. Despondently begin rehabilitation and cross-training.
3. Prematurely and irrationally resume running.
4. One mile in, cause a re-injury and glumly hobble home.
5. Repeat step 2.

Indeed, my alter ego running personality could be equal parts intense and idiotic at times. When that persona would rear its foolish head, my wife would often break out with her rendition of Billy Joel's "I Go to Extremes":

> Darling I don't know why you go to extremes
> Too fast or too slow there ain't no in-betweens
> And if you hurt or you heal
> It's always such a big deal
> Darling I don't know why you go to extremes.

So true. This time would be different, though, because I would avoid repeating all the many mistakes of my past. I'd listen to my knee and know the first sign of diminishing pain wasn't the test signal for a hilly eight-mile run. Fool me once, shame on you; fool me 43 times, well, shame on me.

When my knee was finally pain free, I did the heretofore unthinkable. I waited one more week just to be certain. Mr. Immoderate, meet Mr. Cautious. I then went to the local high school football stadium to do some light jogging on the artificial turf. I've run plenty of races, but my initial pain-free jog across the 100-yard football field was more joyous than any finish line I'd previously crossed. As I ran over the goal line and spiked an imaginary football, I could swear I'd seen angels humming to the harmonious theme music from the movie *Chariots of Fire*, rainbows emerging in the sky, and happy birds flying overhead.

I didn't care that I was running slower than a 70-year-old turtle in sand because the operative word was running. The experience ranked just behind the birth of my children. Okay, perhaps I needed perspective, but jubilation was back in my socks.

In this comeback, I was no longer counting miles per week but yards without pain. Time-honored running wisdom suggests the 10 percent rule: To avoid injury, runners shouldn't increase their mileage more than 10 percent per week. In previous comebacks I'd operated under the more thickheaded 100 percent rule and pretty much doubled my mileage each week. This time I would be the king of caution. I'll see your 10 percent rule and lower you 9 percent. If I'd run 15 miles this week, I'd go up 1 percent a week. Starting with the addition of a whopping 264 yards per week, I figured with compounding mileage, I might get to 50 miles per week about the same time I qualified for Social Security. Whatever, I wouldn't be on the injured list! So what if my weekly mileage in the beginning was equal to my daily mileage in the past? It was still progress. If, as Saint Augustine said, "Patience is the companion of wisdom," then I was now the smartest guy in the locker room.

So my comeback emerged one slow step at a time. Dormant speed eventually emerged, mileage slowly accumulated, and on I went. With signs of discomfort, I pulled back on the throttle. For the first time, I was doing everything the way it was supposed to be done. What a unique concept! An aging runner can learn from past mistakes. To paraphrase philosopher George Santayana, "Those who cannot learn from injury, are doomed to repeat it."

On the injured list.

If I'd run 15 miles this week, I'd go up 1 percent a week. Starting with the addition of a whopping 264 yards per week, I figured with compounding mileage, I might get to 50 miles per week about the same time I qualified for Social Security.

CHAPTER 16

Malady Malfeasance

There are more than two certainties in life

Albert Einstein reportedly said, "Insanity is doing the same thing over and over again and expecting different results." Runners may be nuts, but we're clearly not insane. We may do the same thing over and over, such as pushing the limits of our body too far and incurring an inevitable injury, but the fact is we don't expect a different result. Hey, we're way too smart for that!

We know that remaining injury free is not a forever thing. Although we may take the necessary precautions, none of us is completely immune from a twinge, an ache, or a muscle pull. Runners' injuries are rather predictable. It's not like we will encounter a 380-pound defensive lineman with biceps the size of our waists, ferociously tackling us and trying to twist our lower appendages into a knot and burying them in the turf. Instead, our self-inflicted injuries usually arise from overtraining, overuse, or perhaps a biomechanical flaw in our running motion. We don't even have the bizarre injuries of some professional athletes, like former Washington Redskins quarterback Gus Frerotte who suffered a jammed neck after he head-butted the end zone concrete wall while celebrating a touchdown. Brilliant. We may get shin splints from ramping up the mileage too quickly, but at least we know enough to high-five after a good run rather than bang our head into concrete.

Although, American Olympic sprinter Justin Gatlin recently propelled the running world into the foolish-injury spotlight when his turn in the cryogenic chamber came along. The chamber, which uses liquid nitrogen, rapidly cools muscles after a workout, but apparently certain basic rules should be followed. Namely, don't enter the chamber wearing wet clothing. Gatlin discovered this by incurring frostbite to his toes after entering the chamber wearing sweat-soaked socks, which froze to him instantly. Good thing he wasn't wearing wet running shorts! Gatlin ultimately recovered, but clearly gave new meaning to the term "getting cold feet."

Three forms of rationalization occur when a runner experiences discomfort that most likely can be attributed to a running injury. The first is that no matter the severity of the pain that crops up during a run, a four-word term can describe it: It's just a cramp. We runners could have a compound fracture with our femur in full view, and we'll try to convince ourselves that it's no more than a muscle spasm!

Second, on the day that an injury arrives, we adhere to the unrealistic belief that it will be better in the morning. We consistently try to convince ourselves that nighttime is a miraculous healing world and despite our dramatically limping to bed, we cling to the hope that the *Injury Fairy* will arrive and wave the magical baton and our ailment will be miraculously cured. Guess again, oh optimistic one.

Lastly, there's a phrase uttered by most runners, and I have also uttered it so many times it should eventually be the epitaph on my tombstone: *I think I can run through it*. This is despite the fact that I've yet to incur an ache or pain that actually got better because of a run. The run may momentarily dull the pain, but it will usually return with a vengeance. If I had a dollar for every time I've been

> We runners could have a compound fracture with our femur in full view, and we'll try to convince ourselves that it's no more than a muscle spasm!

required to admit (post run) "That wasn't such a good idea," well let's just say I could afford my own personal 24-hour on-call physician.

Back when I turned 45 years old, I concluded that conversations among Masters runners always migrated toward the topic of each other's injuries. No longer is it the general greeting of "How's your running going?" but the more particular questioning of "Any injuries?" An increased injury rate with age is not necessarily unique to the sport of running. Given that my second love in the sports world is basketball, I played the game at least once a week for most of my adult life. But eventually, my regular hoops game began to resemble an overcrowded MASH unit, and that was before we even began playing. Most players had braces reinforcing every conceivable joint, and we looked more like participants in a game of roller derby than basketball. The games were also moving slower (we gave new meaning to the term "Shuffle Offense"), and as the incidence of injury increased, the attrition factor caused the final buzzer to sound on the game for good.

However, older runners don't just fade away; we run on and eventually become experts in instantly identifying the injuries of others, how long they will take to heal, and the best method of treatment. I can watch a baseball player walk back to the dugout with a distinct limp and am able to immediately diagnose a grade 2 hamstring strain and know exactly how long he'll be on the disabled list. Similarly, I can see a fellow runner come toward me in the grocery store and within four steps, I am able to discern by his or

I can see a fellow runner come toward me in the grocery store and within four steps, I am able to discern by his or her gait whether it's piriformis syndrome with a touch of a calf strain on the opposite side or an illiotibial band problem with a smattering of Achilles tendinitis.

her gait whether it's piriformis syndrome with a touch of a calf strain on the opposite side or an illiotibial band problem with a smattering of Achilles tendinitis. I may not have the smarts to clean up on *Jeopardy!*, but I'd definitely get to the championship round on the game show *Identify That Injury!*

Sure there are ways we can mitigate injuries, but whether we go barefoot or shod, overtrain or undertrain, there's no foolproof repellant for the injury bug that bites us from time to time. We literally and figuratively run the risk of being injured and needing to take time off to heal.

Nonetheless, when an injury does occur, it's like the old Southern phrase "Y'all come back now, y'hear." We hear.

For the love of the game, we will always come back for a comeback.

PART V

From the Back of the Pack to the Fleet Elite, Runners Aren't Run of the Mill

What Some Call Quirks, We Call Talents

CHAPTER 17

If the Shoe Fits, Snare It!

Losing, then rediscovering, your favorite kicks

I could barely believe my eyes as I happened to see the tall figure doing prerace strides across the field. As I kept an eye on his whereabouts, I immediately broke into an all-out sprint over the 200 yards back to my car to grab my wallet. I then dashed back toward him as fast as my legs would carry me.

Without caring in the slightest that I was interrupting his pre-race routine, I waved the wad of cash in my hand and blurted out, "How much for your shoes?"

He just looked at me like I had two heads. I was tense and desperate and shouted, "Seriously man, how much for your shoes?"

He finally said, "What are you talking about?"

I replied with a quaking voice, "I need those shoes, man. I need 'em bad. I'm down to my last pair and then that's it. Nada. Gone forever. I can't take it. I got to have them!"

I pointed down to my dilapidated shoes with the frayed mesh along the top, toes sticking through, worn-out heels, and much duct tape holding various shoe components in place. I pleaded with him, "Look at these! You got to help me, man!"

"Whoa, buddy. Relax. Aren't you even curious what size mine are? What size do you wear?" he asked.

"10 and a half," I replied.

"These are 12 and a half."

"Close enough! I'll wear extra socks. Will you take a credit card?" I screamed.

He waved me away, and I jumped in front of him as he tried to resume his prerace routine. He stared at me with pity in his eyes, placed his hand on my shoulder, and said, "You got to get a grip, buddy."

I didn't need a grip; I needed his Nike Air Zoom Skylons! I longingly stared at his shoes as he jogged off. I imagine he had, figuratively, been in my shoes before. I wanted to at that moment, literally, be in his shoes. If you're a runner long enough, eventually you'll feel the sudden shock of having your perfect running shoe discontinued. Without warning. Extinct. I remember previous running partners experiencing the same frustration when the Saucony Freedom Trainer went down or the Adidas Osweego, the Brooks Radius, the Asics DS Trainer VI, and other shoes meeting their ultimate demise.

I hadn't yet met my perfect shoe until the Skylon came along. I'm not simply referring to a running shoe that fits pretty comfortably. I mean that once-in-a-lifetime, Cinderella glass slipper–like pair that feels as though it's been designed and built just for your foot. The shoe with unreal comfort that produces nary an injury let alone a blister, heel slippage, or even a hint of plantar fasciitis!

When the first version of the Skylon came on the market, it was love at first sight. I put the shoes on, and it was though soft music began playing in the background while rose petals fell from the sky. I took them for a short spin outside, and as I danced down the driveway of the running store, I envisioned long runs together for Skylon and me and years of happiness together. Before indicating to the salesman that I'd take them, I almost felt compelled to say, "I take you to be true in good runs and bad and will love this shoe from this run forward until shoe extinction do us part."

It was indeed inevitable that years down the running road our time to part ways would come. Not because my love would fade, but simply because shoe manufacturers discontinue models and replace them with what they believe to be a better, more technologically advanced shoe. Your all-time favorite abruptly sent to the obsolete-shoe repository.

Before indicating to the salesman that I'd take them, I almost felt compelled to say, "I take you to be true in good runs and bad and will love this shoe from this run forward until shoe extinction do us part."

When the death knell for my Skylon was ringing, I was apparently one of the few devotees that didn't hear it. I'd gone through my last few pairs and went to the local running store to replenish my supply, only to be informed the shoe had been discontinued many months earlier. Frantically screaming, "Noooo!" I immediately ran from the store to uncover all of the remaining pairs in the world.

I was so incensed that I called Nike customer service on the way home and was completely disarmed. They couldn't have been kinder. They steered me in the direction of a few stores throughout the country with Skylons still in stock and suggested comparable shoes. They also delineated Nike's rationale for discontinuing shoes (i.e., innovation, pushing boundaries, a precursor to a new series). They explained why shoes run their course, while I was explaining that I was still on the course and needed my Skylons!

I got home and called the stores they recommended and then jumped to the Internet. Eventually, I stockpiled six pairs in my size, but it was clear I was near the end of my shoe.

I wondered whether there was a cash-only, no-taxes black market for extinct models with no questions allowed as to how the obsolete shoes had been obtained. I imagined my phone ringing in the middle of the night with a muffled voice on the other end saying, "I got a Skylon 10.5. Be at the corner of Church and Vine in 30 minutes. Bring unmarked bills. When you see a guy in a trench coat, whisper 'Shoe in.'"

I imagined my phone ringing in the middle of the night with a muffled voice on the other end saying, "I got a Skylon 10.5. Be at the corner of Church and Vine in 30 minutes. Bring unmarked bills. When you see a guy in a trench coat, whisper, 'Shoe in.'"

Years later, when all my resources had been exhausted (including the guy on the field with his size 12.5s), I conceded to being on my last pair. I savored those shoes as best I could, but the time eventually came when they weren't going to last another 10 yards without disintegrating. My extremely lightweight, durable, and cushioned shoe with Phylite material, super-breathable mesh, natural-motion flex grooves, glovelike fit, extra cushioning in the heel, and an encapsulated and full-length zoom air unit in the midsole with super flexibility had come to its end. Nike Air Zoom Sklyon, RIP.

I buried that last pair in my backyard and the next morning, for the first time in years, I opened a box containing a different model. This pair had many new features that had evolved in running shoe design since my years with the Skylon began. They looked fancy and enticing. But I knew better. I knew there was only one true and magical love for every running sole.

Oh, I'll still date some wonderful shoes in the years to come. But they will never supplant the memories of what my Air Zoom and I had together. In so many ways, the Skylon was right on.

Solemates for eternity.

Running Is Elementary, My Dear

Simplicity is the father of ascension

> Simple pleasures are the last healthy refuge in a complex world.
>
> *Oscar Wilde*

I'm not very complicated. Basic is my middle name. I could eat cereal for dinner my entire life and be more than content. All your daily vitamins with a good dose of fiber in one box, a plethora of choices, and less than one minute and 40 seconds of prep time and with a solitary spoon and one bowl, virtually no cleanup. Homespun and all done.

I'm also a simple guy. Although I know some nonrunners would say that getting up to run at 3:00 a.m. to beat the 114-degree heat while in Las Vegas (although already 94 degrees) makes me more of a simpleton, I'm more into simple fun. Which is the essence of running.

The unadorned nature of running is a big part of what I enjoy about the sport. Its basic tenet is to put one foot in front of the other and repeat, which doesn't challenge my threshold of complicated activities. Running is the anti-complex. These sentiments were also expressed by no less an authority than Barney Stinson from *How I Met Your Mother,* who delineated the basic rules to follow in running a marathon. He said, "Step one, you start running. There is no step two."

> The unadorned nature of running is a big part of what I enjoy about the sport. Its basic tenet is to put one foot in front of the other and repeat, which doesn't challenge my threshold of complicated activities.

Running is the ultimate minimalist activity because there's not a lot in the way of essentials as you head out your door. As I referenced in my first book, other forms of recreation require too many accoutrements, too much planning ahead, or way too much mechanical understanding. Skiing? Mountains weren't usually found within my subdivision. Tennis? You need someone else on the other side of the net or else have incredible speed and agility to play yourself. Tackle football? Shoulder pads, helmets, and 22 people. It's a little difficult to round up a good game before work at 5:30 a.m. Golf? Anything involving a tee time is out from the get-go. The fact that it is often called a thinking person's game is one of the reasons my golf career is limited to trying to crack the timing of the windmill at the local miniature golf course. Having to give thought to which club to use, the grip, the position of my feet and head, my shoulder rotation, my hip rotation, aiming my clubface, my backswing, and so on is about eight things too many for me to digest. When I'm running, I want to ruminate less about what I'm doing and more about everything else. You don't need to think about running, you just get to think while running. It's the ultimate meditation in motion.

Even the relatively simple forms of exercise like bicycling aren't going to work for me because anything involving derailleurs, cranks, or cog sets is outside my area of mechanical knowledge. Plus, I couldn't handle the additional task of equipment maintenance required for a bicycle. I have a hard enough time with the daily maintenance of my body.

It's all about the KISS principle, which is one of my main commandments in life: Keep it simple, stupid. Related to running, I always loved Olympic gold medal marathoner Frank Shorter's response to the question of why he hadn't yet written a book on running. "Why don't I write a book on training? Because it'd be like a page long, that's why." Simple. Doubtful that mini-book would be climbing up the *New York Times* best-seller list.

The act of running is natural and pure, but, admittedly, to some degree it has become much more complex in recent years. Heart rate monitors are intricate and technologically detailed, packed fuel belts resemble aisle 1 of the local 7-Eleven, and it seems you need an electrical engineering degree to figure out how to set the date and time on GPS watches. I usually have difficulty with directions more sophisticated than "You've been provided two labeled pieces: piece 1 and piece 2. Piece 1 resembles a stick and fits into the one and only hole existing on piece 2. Merge the two parts. Assembly is now complete."

I know that plenty of runners enjoy the injection of technology into running. I suppose each to his own, or in this case, each to his own target heart zone. I'll

I'll eschew bringing along a beeping watch or heart rate monitor. I'd prefer the symphony of my footsteps and breathing. I welcome the straightforward while I go straight forward. No frills, all thrills.

eschew bringing along a beeping watch or hear rate monitor. I'd prefer the symphony of my footsteps and breathing. I welcome the straightforward while I go straight forward. No frills, all thrills.

With apologies to Rodgers and Hammerstein, the following, sung to the tune of "My Favorite Things" from *The Sound of Music*, illustrates the simplicity of running:

A light misty rain and the cool runner's high
Getting a great sweat with miles zipping by
Carbo-loading and no aches in hamstrings
These are a few of my favorite things.

Runs in the moonlight and gel at mile 20
Fast runs and grass runs and races a plenty
Gliding along like I feel I have wings
These are a few of my favorite things.

New shoes from the box and blister-free socks
Personal best times on finish line clocks
Soft trails through the woods and smells of the spring
These are a few of my favorite things.

Easy miles on days when it's best to go slow
Cool winter runs on a soft dusting of snow
Going alone and the thoughts that it brings
These are a few of my favorite things.

When the quads hurt
When the shorts chafe
When I've hit the wall
I simply remember all that a run brings
The joy and the fun . . . of it all.

Hey, we may sit on tennis balls to help with piriformis problems and lather petroleum jelly on seemingly random body areas before long runs, and 80 percent of our casual wardrobe may be polyester running shirts, and our freezer may be packed with ice bags. But we're not simpletons.

We're just after simple runs.

CHAPTER

19

Do What They Say, and Watch the Day Zip Away

Operating by the book makes for a long read

As I approached the finish line, the large race clock prominently displayed the rather abysmal news. It was as though the clock, with each second ticking off its huge yellow neon display digits, was mocking me. I swore I heard its heckling voice say, "Are you kidding? Betcha haven't seen these numbers on me in like, well, how many years? No wait, you've never seen these numbers, molasses legs! Nice race, turtle man!"

Yes, this race time was a personal worst. The PW had finally arrived. It was a bit unexpected, but because of my talking acerbic race clock, it cast an indelible memory. Certainly, logic dictated that my performance could be attributed to the relentless nature of Father Time. Ah, that would be too simple, too basic, much too rational. Not my forte.

This result had to be due to something much more unusual. My mind started firing away a series of meager excuses. The hotel's coffee dispenser labels must have been mixed up that morning and I'd been running without caffeine! The initial mile markers were definitely off, causing me to unnecessarily speed my pace and go into severe oxygen debt earlier than usual. The aid station drink was not my normal drink! Oh, I had an endless repertoire of nonsense.

> **What if I actually listened to that little man on my shoe saying, "Do the right thing," when I contemplated whether to stretch or to refuel first after running?**

Over the next few days, my excuse meter went into remission and I tried to more systematically figure out what had gone wrong. I was notorious for pulling out articles from running magazines, dutifully alphabetizing them by subject, and organizing them in a large accordion file. The rather key component I was missing was actually reading the articles!

It is somewhat hard to follow advice without knowing what it actually is. My file of advice regarding pre- and post-running activities was on the verge of exploding when I decided that my recently slower race time meant it was high time to read the articles and adhere to the main suggestions.

I always followed a solid training schedule of many miles and one fartlek and one tempo workout each week. But it was the other roughly 22.5-plus hours in the day that some might say I wasn't taking full advantage of. What if I actually listened to that little man on my shoe saying, "Do the right thing," when I contemplated whether to stretch or to refuel first after running? I figured if it quieted a sarcastic race clock or two in the near future and kept Father Time a while longer at bay, then I was game to try.

It took me about a month, but I read everything and made notes, and I was good to go. Or so I thought. My diary outlining how I spent the entire day doing all the right things follows:

3:45 A.M. Alarm clock sounded and seven minutes later I was astute enough to recall why it was going off 60 minutes earlier than normal! Nutritional experts opined that if a speed workout was on the schedule (and it was) for a morning run, it would be beneficial to awake an hour earlier and eat a small meal to fuel the greater glycogen demand and break the nighttime fast of 10 to 12 hours since one's last meal. I'm fairly certain I've never even chewed gum before 6:00 a.m., but it was now time to scarf down the recommended whole-wheat bagel with low-fat cottage cheese and 16 ounces of sport drink. I somehow got it all down along with my normal cup of coffee (to make me 80 percent coherent) and slowly got dressed while I digested things.

5:15 A.M. My asphalt-covered surroundings were no longer acceptable for running given that most experts recommended softer trails to preserve my joints and assist in recovery from a hard run. One minor problem was living a solid 30-minute drive from the nearest trail. That "do the right thing" little man on my shoe sternly told me to go get the car keys.

6:05 A.M. Sixteen ounces of sport drink and a cup of coffee required one gas station pit stop before arriving at the trailhead. I grabbed a piece of paper from my gym bag. I now had something I'd never had before: a warm-up routine. Although I normally stretched at some point during the day, my morning pre-run routine was to shuffle to the end of the driveway and raise my arms once above my head (with a quick upward glance to make certain I was no longer holding my coffee mug). The articles recommended a tad more to increase my heart rate, get the blood pumping, warm the muscles, open the joints, and increase body temperature.

> My morning pre-run routine was to shuffle to the end of the driveway and raise my arms once above my head (with a quick upward glance to make certain I was no longer holding my coffee mug).

6:06 A.M. First was myofascial release, which sounded a bit like a reverse facelift. Instead, it was a self-massage using The Stick or foam roller. It promotes tissue quality, prevents somatic dysfunction, and releases joint tension. I wasn't sure what it all meant, but I was onboard for quality tissue.

6:10 A.M. Dynamic stretches and muscle-activation mobility drills were next. Sounded like an Army boot camp exercise. Instead, it was a series of controlled movements to stimulate the nervous system and train muscles to warm up. I couldn't train my dog, so I wasn't too sure about my muscles, but after getting up at 3:45 a.m. any bit of stimulation was more than welcome at this point.

So it was arm swings, side bends, hip circles and twists, carioca (no singing involved), pike stretch, knee cradle, swinging leg lifts (only lost my balance four times), forward lunges, reverse lunges with a twist (sounded like a mixed drink), toe walking, heel walking, front grabs (that just didn't sound right), butt kicks (nothing like kicking your own butt first thing in the morning), forward march, backward march (apparently it's best to check your rear view in a park full of trees), and skipping.

6:37 A.M. I did some recommended strides, and by 6:43 the good thing was I'd finally crossed everything off my warm-up list. Bad thing was I definitely felt ready for a nap.

6:45 A.M. For a split second I began walking back to my car to go home when I realized I hadn't done what I was there for. Specifically, run. Whoops! Off I went.

7:58 A.M. I got through the workout all right and the festivities continued. It was time for the cool-down. Previously, this had consisted of spasmodically shaking out my arms and legs as I walked the 17 yards up my driveway. Not exactly the 20 minutes of low-intensity movement that was recommended in the effort to remove lactic acid from my muscles, reduce levels of adrenalin in my blood, and bring my body back to a resting state. I'd already been up for four hours and anything involving a resting state was more than appealing at that point.

But more than just some strides and slow jogging, I had to also engage in jumping jacks (it'd been a solid 40 years since my last side straddle hop), straight-leg shuffles (perfect because I wasn't up for much more than a shuffle), high-knee sprints, towel toe curls, and more skipping among other drills.

8:25 A.M.   It's suggested to consume something very soon after completing a workout to optimize muscle glycogen replacement and enhance recovery. No whole-wheat bagel with low-fat cottage cheese this time around! One of the most recommended recovery foods was a large chocolate milk (given its ratio of carbohydrate to protein). I went to my ice cooler and chugged away along with some fig cookies. A morning that included skipping, jumping jacks, marching, chocolate milk, and cookies brought back fond memories of being 7 years old at summer camp!

9:00 A.M.   Back to the gas station for one more pit stop and cryotherapy. Aptly titled because crying is what I felt like doing after I'd filled with ice the enormous plastic bucket I'd brought and then jumped in thigh high. Ice therapy was to constrict blood vessels, decrease metabolic activity, and reduce swelling and tissue breakdown. I tried not to break down as my lower extremities went numb while sitting in the ice at the side of the gas station. I got my fair share of strange looks with some people wondering whether this was part reality show, part insanity.

9:20 A.M.   After drying off and waiting to thaw so I could actually feel my foot on the car's accelerator, I drove to the gym to do some passive stretching and a 10:00 a.m. Pilates class for posture, flexibility, muscle strengthening, and injury prevention.

> Back to the gas station for one more pit stop and cryotherapy. Aptly titled because crying is what I felt like doing after I'd filled with ice the enormous plastic bucket I'd brought and then jumped in thigh high.

11:00 A.M.   Class was over and I hobbled to the locker room to finally take a shower.

12:00 P.M.   It seemed like it was time for dinner, but I went home and grabbed lunch.

1:00 P.M.   After lunch, the most welcomed activity of the day finally arrived. Naptime. I hadn't taken a scheduled post-meal nap since I was 3 years old, but it was recommended for muscles to recover and the body to reenergize. Who am I to argue?

2:00 P.M. to 5:00 P.M.   I emerged from my slumber and it was on to a packed afternoon of activities including back to the gym for circuit weight training, a killer abdominal workout, additional core muscle building, a late-afternoon cross-training bike ride, a foam-roller routine, and a visit to the chiropractor for manipulation as well as a session of Active Release Technique (ART) on my legs.

6:00 P.M.   I exhaustedly returned home, mumbled some incoherent words to my wife, took another shower, and tried to stay awake during dinner. Afterward, I dragged my body (and sore abs) outside for an evening walk, which was recommended to assist in recovery and prepare for the next morning's run.

8:15 P.M.   I had fallen into a deep sleep on the family room couch, and at 11:00 p.m., I dragged my sore muscles and enervated body upstairs to bed.

The day had zipped by and left me no time for family, work, or anything else besides "doing things the right way." As I crawled into bed (did I mention sore abs?) I unplugged the alarm clock and flung it across the room; 3:45 never again would be a wake-up time for which I volunteered!

Yes, we runners can be compulsive and obsessed at times. As the days went on, I knew that everything in moderation was a more sensible approach with respect to pre- and post-run activities. I did incorporate certain things into my daily running routine, so it was doable and I was actually able to maintain a life outside of running activities.

Most importantly, when I come across the taunting race clock again, I can silence it with a better race result. But, if I don't, I know I can be proud of at least three things. That clock definitely won't be able to heckle me about my towel-toe-curl abilities after a race or my high-knee sprints! Plus, the ability of my legs to withstand frigid temperatures in a bucket is incredible.

Personal worst times, whatever. I've got new talents!

Gesticulate in Kind

To acknowledge or not to acknowledge, that is the question

I've had more than my share of life's embarrassing moments, including one when I was a teenager and had a crush on a girl whom I'd met the prior summer at a cross country camp. Being better with the written word than the spoken word, I opted to express my feelings in a letter to her. I diligently crafted a sincere but not overpowering note and was looking for a little reciprocity in response. When it came time to putting the final touches on my letter, I debated what type of ending salutation to use. Nothing overwhelming like "Love you" or too formal with "Very Truly Yours," or too desperate with "Hope to hear from you soon." Instead I chose something more middle of the road on the affection path. But there was a minor technicality to say the least.

After I didn't receive a response via mail or by phone, I reread my letter. It's then that I noticed a fairly critical typo in my closing salutation. Instead of my chosen ending of "Fondly yours," I had instead astutely typed, "Fondling yours." My bad. I had a better chance of a reply if I'd gone with the more formal "May I always live to serve you and your crown."

Thereafter, I developed a slight salutation phobia not only with letter writing but also with most greetings. Thankfully, when

I began running in the 1970s my concern with proper greetings wasn't a big issue when I encountered other runners on the road. The reason being, back then, there weren't many others out in the early morning except for the newspaper delivery person and squirrels with insomnia.

But as more people gravitated to the sport and I subsequently lived in the running Meccas of Boulder, Colorado, and then Eugene, Oregon, I began encountering numerous runners who crossed paths with mine. Admittedly, I always felt a kindred spirit to other runners, and my salutation phobia wasn't an overwhelming issue with my comrades in carbo-loading and partners in polyester.

I usually acknowledged a fellow runner with a hand wave, a nod, or a simple "Good morning," and customarily received something in kind. But as more and more runners shared the early-morning roads, I quickly learned that not everyone had the inclination to provide a return greeting. In particular, a runner in my neighborhood failed to acknowledge my presence in any way, shape, or form. I realized the lack of reply might not have been caused by rudeness, but perhaps by the runner being in the zone and a meditative state. Nonetheless, like Captain Ahab's quest in *Moby Dick*, it became almost a monomaniacal quest for me to get this runner to at least raise an eyebrow, wink, or even just spit in my general direction.

My quest might have been tilting at windmills, but a nearly imperceptible tilt of the head would have satisfied me. Of course, it would have been easier to simply ask the other runner, "Hey, what's up with no response?" But that would have deprived me of my Captain Ahab–like pursuit.

> Nonetheless, like Captain Ahab's quest in *Moby Dick*, it became almost a monomaniacal quest for me to get this runner to at least raise an eyebrow, wink, or even just spit in my general direction.

So I'd hit the roads each morning armed in my mind with not only my planned workout but also a new greeting or two to try out should my path intersect that of my rather reticent runner. I tried a gentle "Hey," the more hip "Yo, Homey," and a quick "'Sup?" I received not even a sideways glance. I next concluded that perhaps the runner had recently moved from another country and didn't speak much English. So on a few mornings, I took a stab at different languages, beginning with "Hola" and progressing through "Bonjour," "Ni Hao," and "Guten Tag" among others. I got not even a "Ciao" or "Shalom" in return.

I then went the nonverbal route and proceeded through doffing my running cap, giving a thumbs-up, and saluting and still nada in return. Eventually, I stopped encountering the non-communicative one. Perhaps the runner had altered the course thinking that I was, in my ongoing effort to generate a response, just one step away from mooning.

But years of greeting other runners enables me to conclude there are vastly more people who wave, nod, and so on than those who do not. I also recall the first time I ran in New York City's Central Park where let's just say the loneliness of the long distance runner is rather nonexistent. I felt pretty much like the Queen of England, with a perpetual wave throughout my run. My only muscle soreness the next morning was in my right arm.

There are some running etiquette issues that arise when greeting a fellow runner. What about when you encounter slower runners going in the same direction you are? As you pass them, do you turn around and acknowledge them or are you thereby reinforcing the reality of their much slower pace? Or is it disrespectful to provide no form of hello? I'd lean toward providing a greeting other than the mocking "Meep, meep," cartoon greeting as the speedy Road Runner passes Wile E. Coyote.

And what do you do at a local race on an out-and-back course where you're zeroed into your competitive groove? You've reached the turnaround and are heading back toward the start while so many other runners that you know are still coming toward you. Do you high-five everyone you know, or does that expend too much energy and take you out of your zone? Do you run the risk of an overexuberant friend fist bumping with too much force and impacting not only your knuckles but your finish time as well? If oncoming friends cheer you, do you reciprocate and waste precious oxygen shouting out encouragement for them also? So many prerace considerations beyond what's my goal pace and are my shoelaces tight enough and double tied.

Or is it disrespectful to provide no form of hello? I'd lean toward providing a greeting other than the mocking "Meep, meep," cartoon greeting as the speedy Road Runner passes Wile E. Coyote.

And if I ever cross paths with my old non-responsive neighborhood runner? Well, perhaps I'll just offer an ambivalent body shrug in exchange for the cold shoulder. No need to wind up like Captain Ahab.

Also, because I know that with the plethora of more demonstrative runners on the road these days, a greeting in the form of a return wave or virtual collective hug is likely to be just around the corner.

I can run with that.

The Nonthinker's Guide to the Path of Least Resistance

Yoda says, "Do or Do Not. There Is No Try"

CHAPTER 21

Do What You Want to Do

Whatever starts your engine and puts a bounce in your step

Simply the thing that I am shall make me live.

William Shakespeare

I recently read the comments of tennis great Serena Williams in describing her passion, or rather lack thereof, for her sport, an activity that she has devoted a great portion of her life toward being the best she could be. And she's done it amazingly well. In a Jan. 2, 2012, article on www.tennisnow.com, Williams said the following:

> "It's not that I've fallen out of love (with tennis), I've actually never liked sports, and I never understood how I became an athlete. I don't like working out, I don't like anything that has to do with working physically. If it involves sitting down or shopping, I'm excellent at it."

Three things quickly came to mind in digesting her words. First, because I break out in hives upon stepping into malls given my aversion to shopping, Serena and I are on opposite sides of the emporium. Second, I work standing up at a raised desktop and can't sit still for much more than the opening credits to a sitcom, so Serena and I wouldn't be perched together on the same sofa for very long. Last, like most runners, I love working out, so Serena doesn't exactly share our view that sweat is the raison d'être.

But Serena obviously gets a certain amount of satisfaction from tennis, be it winning Grand Slam championships, the economic remunerations, the fame, or something else. She may not truly enjoy the act of playing tennis or the physical effort in maintaining her elite level, but she must enjoy enough of what it provides to keep doing it. I know there are runners who don't really adore the activity of running, but they do enjoy other things that it brings them. Be it camaraderie, competition, weight loss, or health benefits. I know runners whose feeling toward running is akin to the old joke:

> Why do you beat your head against the wall?
> Because it feels so good when I stop!

We have many reasons for choosing to be runners, and often nonrunners don't understand our enjoyment at all. Along these lines, a popular T-shirt has a picture of a runner and the saying "My sport is your sport's punishment." That is how some athletes in other sports view running. A 300-pound football player is going to get as much joy out of running laps as I would in trying to tackle a running back who has a full head of steam and thighs bigger than my waist. We gravitate toward what we enjoy and what provides a measure of success. Running legend Steve Prefontaine had his own athletic epiphany. He played football in school until he realized that as a sub-100-pound running back, he'd have more success becoming a sub-4:00 miler. And he did (and smartly avoided getting flattened by a linebacker in the process).

The fact is that people do what they want to do, which is why it always struck me as incongruous to label an event as a "Fun Run" or to label a subset of runners as "fun runners." If you aren't having fun while devoting yourself to running, then you really shouldn't be doing it. Thus, we're all fun runners in one capacity or another. We all may have different reasons for running: the highly competitive racer, the back of the packer, and the 70-mile-per-week runner doing it solely for the joy of the physical act of running. The bottom line is if running doesn't float your boat, then you best discover what else will keep you afloat.

Some people enjoy mountain climbing or jumping out of airplanes or riding roller coasters. I don't. I'm quite content with the exhilaration and rush of riding the wooden horses on the merry-go-round along with the preschool crowd. But I don't need to question why someone would volunteer to drop in a steel car at speeds over 95 miles per hour from a height longer than a football field and a vertical angle of nearly 100 degrees, all while screaming at the top of their lungs. They do it because they want to. Simple. And we run because we want to, because we need to, because we enjoy it. It's basic human desire and you really don't get a whole lot more basic than putting one foot in front of the other and moving quickly.

Each of us continues to be a runner for a variety of reasons. For many it's like Roger Bannister (the first runner to break four minutes in the mile) said, "We run, not because we think it is doing us good, but because we enjoy it and cannot help ourselves." For others it might partly be a bittersweet relationship, an action we may not terribly enjoy but a sacrifice we make for other things we do like about running. Award-winning author (and runner) Joyce Carol Oates summed it up nicely in a July 18, 1999, essay in the *New York Times* by pretty much encompassing, in one sentence, all the various reasons why we run: "On days when I can't run, I don't feel 'myself'; and whoever the 'self' is I feel, I don't like nearly so much as the other."

The famous soul-singing group the Isley Brothers summed it up like this:

It's your thing, do what you wanna do.
I can't tell you, who to sock it to.

Similarly, as others try to determine which type of physical activity best rocks their socks, I can't tell them what exercise to sock it to. They'll have to figure it out just like we runners figured out that putting a sock and foot into a running shoe worked best for us.

If, for whatever reason, my running days come to a close, then I'm going to miss it a heck of a lot more than Serena Williams is going to miss tennis. I'll obviously be sad, but I will look back with enjoyable memories and say, "It's been a good run."

And I did what I wanted to do.

CHAPTER 22

Giving Yourself the Benefit of No Doubt

Sometimes it's best to just stop thinking

Before my son's first middle school football game, he was overly concerned about catching the ball, which was predetermined to be thrown to him on the first play. My wife, who couldn't care less if he caught it or not, provided maternal words of encouragement regarding how it didn't matter: Don't worry, your teammates and coaches won't get upset, just have fun, you'll do fine, it's all about enjoyment, and so on. I concluded he was overthinking things and needed soothing paternal advice. What actually came out was more like Commandant Caustic as I sternly said in a vexed voice, "Just catch the damn ball, Son!"

Okay, perhaps not my finest moment as a parent, but he got the drift, actually relaxed a bit, and gained some confidence that it could be done. The sentence ultimately became a humorous part of our family lexicon and carried influence. Years later, my 12-year-old daughter was getting extremely nervous before a competitive dance routine and was psyching herself out by watching her very skilled competitors warm up. I looked into her eyes and she then said to me, "Is this a 'Just catch the damn ball' moment, Dad?" It was indeed, and she relaxed, stopped overthinking and figuratively caught the ball.

That's how it is to me with running. Sometimes we overthink things, be it because of prerace jitters or fearing a difficult workout or wrestling with whether to go for a run as we listen from our bed to the early-morning howling winds and the fierce rain. More than 20 years ago Nike put forth the three words that have become a part of the physical fitness world: "Just do it." Tantamount to "Just catch the damn ball!" I don't think of the option of not going for a run. "Just do it" is a call to action with no room for the involvement of thinking, which is often perfectly natural for me. It's amazing what I can accomplish when I don't put my mind to it.

Sticking with the slogan theme and paraphrasing Taco Bell's mantra, I don't "Think outside the run." I just don't think at all about going for a run, not going for a run, shortening the run, and so on. Just catch the damn ball. In essence, if the internal debate of going or not going for a run doesn't even enter my head, then not going is never a choice. I give myself the benefit of no doubt. It is my evenhanded and empty-headed approach to getting out the door. I refuse to even answer Microsoft's advertisement question of "Where do you want to go today?" given that the options would include going back to sleep or to the doughnut shop. Just run.

> "Just do it" is a call to action with no room for the involvement of thinking, which is often perfectly natural for me. It's amazing what I can accomplish when I don't put my mind to it.

On days when I'm tired or the weather is punishing, I know that once I'm outside, a run is going to be well worth it and I'll feel much better after running than if I had lain in bed. I'd rather follow Nike's principle of "Just do it" than to have my window of opportunity close on going for a run and then hearing that little man on my shoulder saying you "Just blew it." It's what I want to do even though there are definitely runs where I feel half asleep at the beginning and start off slow enough that I could easily be rear-ended by a sleep-deprived tortoise.

On those less-than-energetic mornings, my brain synapses begin to kick in around mile one. My first coherent thought is usually one of hoping I actually had the wherewithal to put my running shorts on before leaving the house. As Karl Malden said regarding American Express Travelers Cheques, "Don't leave home without them."

Other company catchphrases can easily be applied to running. Mazda referenced "A passion for the road," which is clearly what runners possess and Royal Caribbean, the cruise line, presented a theme similar to "Just do it" with "Get out there."

When our non-running neighbors see us consistently cruise by, they may think of the indefatigable Energizer Bunny who "keeps going and going and going." There's also the question posed by Rolaids, "How do you spell relief?" and the answer for runners is often two words: Finish line.

I never imagined I'd actually quote a perfume ad, but one that runners can definitely relate to is Calvin Klein's, which states, "Between love and madness lies obsession," a tagline that is an apropos description of many a runner's relationship with running. Possibly the short phrase that best describes the passion runners feel toward running is one that's been around the longest: Coca Cola's "It's the real thing." Indeed it is.

With respect to running, I adhere to Dannon Yogurt's advice of "Love it for life," but perhaps there is another reason I don't ever think of not going for a run. I don't want my children to ever catch me staring blankly outside with running shoes in hand and detect a sign of vacillation. Because I know exactly what would happen if that occurred.

They wouldn't be able to get the words out of their mouth fast enough: "Just catch the damn ball, Dad!"

CHAPTER 23

More Than a Feeling

Take to the sky on a natural high

This isn't my sanctimonious moment. I have my share of less-than-laudable quirks. But I am a lifelong teetotaler and have never smoked anything other than overcooking microwave popcorn, and my mushroom ingestion is button tops and not the magic or psychedelic kind. Coincidentally, though, I have put sautéed mushrooms on my popcorn. (Told you I had my share of eccentricities.)

The only highs I've experienced come from the euphoria of a great run and also by devouring of an entire container of French silk ice cream. The frozen dessert feat is much more hallucinogenic and incapacitating than a runner's high. It produces a surge of energy and then a stupor similar to having done way too many 400-meter intervals. The latter is to *feel the burn* and the former is to *feel the churn*.

A significant difference occurs in obtaining a runner's high and the sugar high after intensely scraping the bottom of the ice cream container. There's a direct cause and effect with the latter, an ability to produce initially energetic feelings after the creamery consumption. Most of my runs provide me with that anticipated and joyful "Wow, that felt pretty good!" emotion. But as far as being able to produce the more elusive, unmitigated, and transcendent runner's high experience, well, its occurrence is about as easy to predict as the exact number of miles you'll run over the next decade.

The focused, calm, and vital feeling that occurs with my daily runs is more a constant companion than the intermittent guest of the runner's high. My daily run has been one of my closest friends for over 40 years. It's helped me solve problems, guided me to some great ideas (as well as some ridiculous ones), accompanied me to the heights of ecstasy, and has humbled me on many occasions. It's been there after births and after deaths, after joy and after sorrow. But over my long running career, I can recall only a handful of times that I've gone beyond the more standard "in the zone" type of feeling and experienced a true runner's high. Those few occasions have left me with blissful elation, experiencing a running rhapsody as though gliding on air with a flowing, effortless, and exultant feeling. I'm at one with my shoes! Okay, perhaps a bit too metaphysically spiritual, but you get my drift. And with running, we get its gift.

If a magical runner's high were less elusive and more an easily occurring daily event, then our streets would be jam-packed by hordes of runners with rapturous feelings of euphoria plastered all over their excited faces. But we run for many different reasons besides the elusive quest for the Holy Grail or, more aptly, the Holy Trail.

Scientists have long studied running's neurochemical effects on the brain, and the feelings produced by running, even well short of a true runner's high, have generated much current debate. That discussion centers on whether the mood-altering chemicals released during running are endorphins or, perhaps, are endocannabinoids (natural compounds within our body that are essentially identical to those found in cannabis). If that be true, can you imagine if legendary reggae singer and Rastafarian Bob Marley were also a runner? Talk about a perpetual state of serenity.

All this said regarding the ecstasy that running can bring, I always wondered what would happen if that sublime joy were abruptly taken away from me. And then it happened. No need to wonder. A tidal wave of injury rolled in, one that placed me on the sidelines for about nine months. I immediately feared my personality would become that of a foaming rabid dog and I'd enter a world of perpetually dark despair while engaging in an incessant pity party.

I figured that nothing would match the feelings produced by running. But I was wrong. No, I didn't start ingesting those previously referenced magic mushrooms but adapted to the necessity of a completely different workout routine. I readily admit that nothing occurred that was similar to the extreme emotions of a runner's high. However, an invigorating indoor nonimpact cardio workout at the local gym could provide sweat-induced feelings of euphoria similar to those of running. All this despite a setting of artificial lights, piped-in dance music overhead that wasn't exactly on my playlist, and the jolting cacophony of free weights colliding on barbells. In such a setting, who'd have thunk that I could subdue my nonrunning funk?

Did I wish I could run? Darn right. But, after so many years of running, I actually learned I could survive without it (although I really, really preferred not to). It was like someone had taken away my French Silk ice cream and substituted Rocky Road. Not as tasty, but very good nonetheless. Maybe it wasn't the running after all. Maybe it was just the exercise-induced, heart-pounding exhilaration and puddles of perspiration that I loved and it didn't really matter the source. Or did it?

As I returned to running, I slowly realized there was something different on the roads compared to what I'd experienced during other workouts while injured. Running was like meeting an old friend and easily resuming a relationship after time apart. I welcomed returning to the solitude of early-morning runs, the feeling of self-propelled movement, the beauty of soft dirt trails, and the concreteness of what a mile's pace signified. Oh sure, running isn't all sunshine and daffodils. There are aches and pains and days when my legs feel like they're stuck in quicksand while each mile seems to last longer than the time it takes to read *War and Peace*.

But those days are very few and far between. I'll continue to enjoy the daily feel-good aspect of running as long as I'm able, all the while knowing the mysteriously elusive runner's high may not come around more than once a decade. I'll also keep in the back of my mind that I can survive if the day should come when injuries prevent me from running anymore.

I just don't think that *I Elliptical, Therefore I Am—NUTS!* has quite the same ring to it.

The Time Is Now

Times may be a-changing, but our infatuation with time is constant

Olympic gold medalist Frank Shorter once said, "You have to forget your last marathon before you try another. Your mind can't know what's coming." Which is why I'm convinced that in a glycogen depleted state with a dazed look and ambulation slower than a teetering toddler, the most prevalent postmarathon question is "Why do I keep doing this?"

Eventually, a more lucid postrace question always emerges among runners: "What was your time?" Nonrunners will even pose this question, although they may be completely unaware of the difference between the marathon wall and Pink Floyd's best-selling album *The Wall*.

Most runners become obsessed with the many facets of time because its variations permeate much of our running world. We've tried to *bank time* in the first half of a race (like that ever works as it usually produces *bonk time* at some point in the second half. Not recommended for the faint of heart). We're familiar with terminology such as *chip time*, *gun time*, *finish time*, *split time*, *personal record time*, and *MPM time* (minutes per mile). We know about running tangents to *save time*, and we've memorized Boston Marathon *qualifying times* for our age divisions over the next 30 years. We know our exact *pace-per-mile time* for our *goal race time*, and from *time to time* we've experienced the difficulty of having *no time* to fit in a daily run. We know specific times so well that if we're awakened from a deep slumber in the middle of the night, we may not be coherent enough to recite our last name but can easily spit out our *personal best times* from a 5K to a marathon.

Idioms and phrases involving time are as common to running as is a race aid station at mile 20. It's like the athletes who are unaware that they constantly pepper their postgame interviews with the ubiquitous "you know." Our running commentary often involves the word *time*, even though we may not realize it occurs almost *all the time*. So it's *high time* we looked at the ways that common phrases involving *time* fit into our running world. For the *time being*, this is what I have:

We've experienced those magical races where we feel indefatigable, effortlessly gliding along at race pace and assured that *time is on our side*. Similarly, when we finally have a breakthrough race performance, we confidently knew it was just a *matter of time* (both literally and figuratively). And if we have a bad patch in a race but subsequently feel better, then we desperately try to *make up for lost time*.

From *time to time*, we need to shake up our training, knowing *it's time* for a change

> Our running commentary often involves the word *time*, even though we may not realize it occurs almost *all the time*. So it's *high time* we looked at the ways that common phrases involving *time* fit into our running world.

to prevent becoming stale. This may include implementing shorter interval work that leaves us feeling like we have *little time to recover* or *time to breathe* but will eventually improve our speed *in time*. You'll enjoy having an *easier time* of it with the next day's slow recovery run. And we've read about junk miles being a *waste of time*, which may produce injury and cause us to *lose time* in the end.

Coming back from an injury, we have to be content with taking it *one day at a time* and avoid returning to running too quickly because *time does heal all wounds*. If we do otherwise, we run the risk of reinjury and then spending considerable *time off* from running.

We welcome races where the *time is right* and we confidently arrive at the starting line with months of solid injury-free training, primed to run a great race on a day with perfect weather and a tailwind. We appreciate in more ways than one how *timing is everything*.

We know that to run negative splits, it's best to *bide your time* in the first half of the race to be *right on time* the second half. Otherwise, going out too fast will result in an incredibly *rough time* for you, and postrace words of attempted solace from your running partners will include "You'll get 'em *next time.*"

When we're running by a crowded golf course and looking at the golfers waiting to tee off, we know we have much *better things to do with our time* than that. And we do, because running is providing us *the time of our life*. With all of its mental and physical benefits, we know that by running we're *spending our time wisely*.

While waiting in our driveway for our late-arriving running partner, we impatiently check our watch knowing that *time's a wasting*. Finally, he arrives and it's *time to hit the road*. And those training runs with our running group where the conversation flows effortlessly and enjoyably, leave us at the end thinking how *time sure flies when we're having fun*. Conversely, when we're putting in a long run alone, it may feel that *time seems to drag on*.

When the very popular races now fill up within milliseconds of being open for registration, we note that it's simply a *sign of the times* and the way races are *for the time being*.

When we're feeling poor during a race, we're grateful when we see either a finish line, port-a-potty, or aid station just *in the nick of time*, and *many times* we've hit the wall and feel like we're *living on borrowed time*. We make certain that our shoelaces are knotted securely before a race so we don't *lose precious time* tending to a loose lace, and we always try to hit the bathroom *one last time* before the gun goes off.

We've spent many out-of-town race weekends *passing time* and anxiously awaiting that *point in time* in which the race begins. When it finally does, we excitedly note that *it's about time* (in more ways than one) and there's *no time like the present*. We've also had those less-than-stellar races where we do calculations over the last stages to determine whether we can still meet our *goal time* as we realize that, in more ways than one, *time is running out*.

> We've also had those less-than-stellar races where we do calculations over the last stages to determine whether we can still meet our *goal time* as we realize that, in more ways than one, *time is running out*.

Our races are mostly a *race against time*. However, on those occasions where we're running on beautiful and scenic courses and are less concerned with how fast we run and more with *taking time to smell the roses*, we can concisely answer the ever present question of "*What was your time?*" We can simply respond with "Not sure, but I know I had a *great time*."

In the end, we know that any run is *time well spent*, and even when races or training runs don't turn out as we had hoped, we will keep coming back for another run.

Time and time again.

PART

VII

The Loneliness of the Long- Distance Nonrunner

Weak in the Knees While Knee Deep in Anatomy

Woe Is Knee!

An inability to run a step is the first step to admitting you have a problem

My college-age son handed me my birthday present, and as I peeled the packaging away, an amused and excited smile came to my face. There, inside the box, was the one thing that had captivated and mesmerized me over the past year. It was the sole entity that I'd read more about than any topic during my running career. I'd also come to recognize it as the gatekeeper of what lay in store for my future running days. I removed the gift from the box and, lo and behold, I held in my hand my right knee. Well all right, not exactly my knee per se, but a large 3D anatomical model of a remarkably healthy-appearing knee. I was finally able to play with a detachable ligament system, glide my fingers across a smooth medial meniscus, caress the tibial tuberosity, and touch a lateral epicondyle. All of which I had theretofore only dreamt about!

With this physiologically movable plastic joint, I could produce abduction, anteversion, retroversion, and so much more. This was greater than the excitement of a kid in a candy store or even a runner at a huge race expo. This was a runner in anatomy class, long-distance guy in pathology lab. I was in obsessed-injured-runner and amateur-doctor heaven!

I carried it around with me all day, put it on my dashboard when I drove to the store, gave it its own seat at the dinner table, and placed it next to me, on my nightstand when I went to bed. I think my dog was actually jealous.

A year earlier, I hadn't known my meniscus from an abacus, but like most runners battling a nagging injury, I became quite educated regarding my malady. At this point, it was clear I'd produced a solid "woe is knee" issue.

If you've read a couple of the previous chapters of this book that touch on my right-knee problem, then you're aware that it ultimately healed (at least I thought it had), and I resumed running. But, not so fast, Mr. Medial Collateral Ligament Man. The road to recovery I was on was Boomerang Boulevard. I'd eventually find myself returning to the starting line and beginning again on my personal avenue to exasperation.

Like any other compulsive runner, I kept searching for the answer and followed up with three other eminently qualified orthopedic surgeons, but things never improved. However, as I held my new anatomical plastic-knee friend, I was certain I'd accurately diagnosed the cause of my pain as being a horizontal tear of the posterior horn in my medial meniscus. Although this sounded akin to guessing the answer in

> The road to recovery I was on was Boomerang Boulevard. I'd eventually find myself returning to the starting line and beginning again on my personal avenue to exasperation.

the board game Clue, it wasn't a shot in the dark. Admittedly, my comprehensive and state-of-the-art MRI months back had detected nothing significant in the medial area of my knee, but why let modern technology stand in the way of a good diagnosis?

I'd been prescribed physical therapy, hip X-rays, heavy doses of anti-inflammatory medication, and stretching exercises. I'd been advised to stop cross-training and completely rest the knee (okay, maniacal runners are not exactly the poster children for patient compliance) and I was also callously told that it was time to consider giving up running altogether. That physician examination was quickly aborted as I shot an incredulous look and indignantly limped out stage left with a muffled suggestion that he should consider giving up orthopedics altogether. Somehow, *I Used to Run, Therefore I Was—NUTS!* just didn't seem like it would have the same allure to a potential running reader.

Holding my anatomical model of the knee securely in my hands, I was a shining example of how a little knowledge can be a dangerous thing with runners. With my overestimated medical wisdom, I concluded it was time for another MRI and surgery was on the horizon. Of course, one minor technicality was that I had to get an actual physician to agree with my diagnosis because I hadn't yet mastered the surgical thing, despite my new hobby of spending mind-numbing hours watching videos of knee arthroscopies online. Yes, I'd now gone 180 degrees from my previous philosophy of "no tubelike fiber-optic scoping instrument will come within a marathon's distance of my skin" to "Can I get an orthopedic surgeon in here, please?"

> I'd now gone 180 degrees from my previous philosophy of "no tubelike fiber-optic scoping instrument will come within a marathon's distance of my skin" to "Can I get an orthopedic surgeon in here, please?"

So I grabbed my anatomical knee friend for security and hobbled back to Dr. Number One, and politely persuaded him to order another MRI. The next day I had a return engagement with those terribly confusing patient gowns and the hollow cylinder magnetic machine with the booming noises. I got to lie perfectly still (not my forte) for a seemingly endless period while the nuclei in my atoms were rearranged. What could be more fun on a Saturday afternoon?

When the report was eventually faxed to me, I read it alongside my anatomical model buddy and quickly concluded I'd developed nearly every abnormality that could possibly inflict a runner's knee. The next day my doctor talked me off the ledge and assured me that not everything noted was cause for concern. Thankfully, he agreed with my diagnosis of a degenerative tear in my medial meniscus and surgery was the most viable option. It's always good to have a concurring opinion from someone who actually has access to a surgical suite, can provide an anesthesiologist, and has successfully introduced a flexible fiber-optic scope into a joint a few thousand times.

I was now welcoming another crack (no pun intended) at mastering one of those patient gowns and having arthroscopic surgery to address my issue. There was finally a true game plan in place for my knee and, in the distance, an actual finish line on the road to recovery.

But the most important question had not yet been answered. Not how soon I might be running again or is it asking too much to bring an upper-body ergometer into the recovery room for a quick postsurgical workout. No, the most important question was whether I could take a good luck charm into surgery: my new best friend in the land of plastic lower-leg anatomical models.

My doctor humored me and gave me the green light. But I also realized my relationship with my inanimate knee might just wane in the near future if I was given the opportunity to watch my surgery live on a video screen. I'd imagine that for any runner who's clearly seen his own meniscus, articular cartilage, and medial collateral ligament up close and personal on the big screen, well plastic replicas might just not do it anymore. I wouldn't discard mine though, like some summer romance.

I could always use a large anatomical reference tool as a dashboard ornament. What obsessed runner wouldn't?

The Arms Have It

*"You'll have to stop weight-bearing exercise for a while."
A survivor's tale*

Many runners enjoy the purity of our sport and run without modern technological accoutrements such as a running watch, headphones and music, and heart rate monitors. Heck, some runners have further advanced the bare-necessity approach and have removed one-third of the running trinity of shorts, shirt, and shoes. Thankfully, it's not the shorts; they've instead chosen to relegate their running shoes to superfluous status.

However, one area exists in which all runners appreciate the benefits that technology has provided. When pesky injuries arise and we're searching for greener endorphin pastures, we're pleased with the availability of many cross-training modalities that significantly elevate our heart rate just thinking about them. We have the elliptical, the recumbent stationary bicycle, high-tech rowing machines, stair climbers, and even the relatively expensive but effective antigravity treadmill (and what I wouldn't give for a little antigravity at the end of some of my long runs).

I've taken advantage of most of the challenging forms of mechanical masochism when I haven't been physically able to put in the miles and needed a substitute for running. These cross-training apparatuses have one thing in common, besides producing such profuse perspiration that other people avoid machines next to me for fear of an unwelcome shower.

What is universal among almost all cross-training exercise equipment is that it requires the predominant involvement of our legs. Let's be honest, most runners don't devote a whole lot of attention to the size of their deltoids or the endurance of their triceps. A steady diet of long-distance running produces biceps more akin to Olive Oyl's than Popeye's, and it's relatively clear that even elite runners aren't going to win too many arm wrestling contests. Our arms would really only come into play in a race if we were crawling to the finishing line after hitting the wall or pushing someone out of the way in a mad scramble for the last cinnamon raisin bagel at the postrace refreshments.

Certainly we need our arms for balance, and they do move in tandem with our gait and assist in our economy of motion. However, it's fair to say that our arms are not exactly our strength. So it's not unusual that most runners' cross-training machines of choice don't involve our biceps. The difficulty for me arose when I learned I needed knee surgery and was not going to be able to bear weight on my right leg for a while. I had to uncover new ways of achieving my daily dose of sweat, stopping short of sitting in a sauna for long stretches or elevating my heart rate by consuming a steady flow of quintuple espressos.

Kayaking or canoeing might work, but because this was during the middle of winter in the Midwest, that wasn't a feasible option. As runners, we've witnessed wheelchair athletes at races and their prodigious talents. They often train with exercise equipment that focuses on their upper body, including hand ergometers, or Krankcycles, but this equipment was not available at my local fitness center and to obtain an arms-only machine for a limited time, well, I wasn't willing to pay an arm and a leg. I could have tried circuit training, but going as fast as possible from weight machine to weight machine while on crutches just might not have been the best postoperative plan.

My research at the fitness center had left me empty handed. Continuing with the appendage idioms, I didn't quite have a leg up on this arms-only exercise thing. I was stressed out over how to stress out my body via exercise (using only my arms) when it dawned on me. I needed to think outside the socks.

I was willing to try my hand (or arms) at anything and concluded I needed to see whether exercise machines could be used in a different manner than they were designed for. Runners can be a resourceful bunch when searching for an endorphin fix, and desperate times were now calling for desperate measures. We all know that injured runners gotta do what injured runners gotta to do.

I first eliminated the idea of lying face down on the fitness center floor in front of a stationary bicycle while reaching up to grab the bike's pedals and creating my own arm ergometer. I tried it out but garnered too many people stepping on my back as I lay across the aisle. Plus my view from down there wasn't exactly the greatest, and let's just say a gym floor isn't the most sanitary place in town.

After circling the row of elliptical machines, the proverbial light bulb finally went off. I realized that if I stood at the front of the machine (facing the elliptical and chest against the back of the display monitor), I could reach over to grab the arm handles and use them without involving my legs. My quest was over. I was no longer empty handed.

I tried it out for a bit and all was good. I'd be ready when my time for non-weight-bearing activity arrived. One word of warning, though, if you find yourself in the same boat. Make sure you position your legs so the foot pedals (minus your feet) don't smash into your kneecaps as the pedals swing forward. Colliding with a rapidly moving piece of steel "knee-on" is not exactly what you're looking for after surgery.

Let's just say my novel elliptical machine approach garnered more than my fair share of stares, accompanied by a "Really now?" expression. Many onlookers were obviously questioning my sanity as they politely tried to instruct me I was using the machine the wrong way. They were obviously not experienced with injured fanatical runners or they would have immediately understood our determined (albeit peculiar) mindset. The runners at the fitness center would give me an approving nod as they strode by. They understood. Hands down.

My arms-only workout served its cardiac conditioning purpose while my knee healed. Hopefully, I won't again be in the position of looking for non-weight-bearing exercise. But if it does come to pass, I know I could return to my novel approach with the elliptical.

With open arms.

CHAPTER 27

Scope Me Out

"A man's got to know his limitations." —Dirty Harry

I can handle my own pain. That's what most runners are able to do. However, I exhibit a weak stomach when it comes to witnessing the pain or injury of others. Push through the nauseatingly latter stages of a marathon with a stress fracture in my ankle? No problem. Been there, done that. See my own blood-soaked socks from blisters run amok? Not an issue. Feel the blinding pain of a piece of my meniscus getting caught within my knee joint? That can now stoically be checked off my anatomical lowlights list.

I'm a wee bit weaker when it's someone else holding the pain barometer. Witnessing NFL quarterback Joe Theismann sustain an open fracture of both his tibia and fibula on live television? I had nightmares for weeks and could barely look at my lower leg for the next year and a half. Watching triathlon great Paula Newby-Fraser collapse 200 feet from the finish line at the 1995 Hawaii Ironman and painfully struggle for 22 minutes before dragging herself across the finish line? I needed to rehydrate and lie down after viewing that one because I felt like I was the one who bonked. Witness my wife undergo a cesarean section? My first recollection as a father was regaining consciousness in another room, sipping apple juice while a nurse asked, "Can you hear me?" Not quite how I anticipated the beginning of parenthood.

So when it came time for surgery on my meniscus, I was ready and prepared to handle it. It was, after all, my body and those types of things I could usually always stomach. I was even certain I could remain awake during the procedure and watch it on the monitor in the operating room without getting queasy and passing out. Well, choose again, Mr. Weak in the Knees.

As runners, we're confronted with choices all the time. There are the basic ones like are you getting out the door today and, if so, how far and how fast? We encounter choices regarding what race pace we should shoot for and when we should begin our taper, and we choose between going with a minimalist shoe or fully cushioned or something in between. We choose how many intervals to do and what kind of shape we'll be in down the road as we choose between pre-registering for the marathon or the half. We know ourselves best and try to make conscious choices based on our experience, abilities, and limitations. I thought I knew my abilities and limitations with respect to my surgery, but my experience in that arena was about the same as my experience with bungee jumping naked in an ice storm. In other words, nonexistent.

> I thought I knew my abilities and limitations with respect to my surgery, but my experience in that arena was about the same as my experience with bungee jumping naked in an ice storm. In other words, nonexistent.

The beauty of running is that we can, at times, modify a choice when we subsequently determine our aspirations might need to be toned down or even moved up a bit. A 20-mile training run may end at 16 miles if we're feeling extremely ill. Or, at some point during a race, we may choose to pick up our goal pace a little if we're feeling super strong that day. The differences between conscious running choices and other choices involving things like, say, arthroscopic surgery are that we can often alter the former midstream. Not so easy to do with the latter when the doctor is about to insert small surgical instruments into your body. It's not exactly the best time to say, "You know, on second thought . . ."

All of this dawned on me when the anesthesiologist entered my surgical prep room. I suddenly wondered whether I'd overestimated my earlier decision to be as alert as possible during the procedure and receive a spinal anesthetic. My earlier thinking had been how many of us can actually raise our hand at having seen our meniscus, synovial tissue, and articular cartilage all up there on the video screen? How many times would I get a chance for a front-row seat on the operating table to observe inside my knee joint? Not many I hoped, so at that time I wanted to be one of the chosen view!

But, come game day, I went from my choice of spinal anesthesia to being put to sleep with a general anesthetic faster than you can say, "See you in postop recovery, Doc."

The change in heart was my faint of heart. I'd actually felt nauseated after witnessing the nurse simply shaving my knee area. Not exactly the most invasive procedure to stomach, so if the sight of a bald patella made me break out in a cold sweat, then maybe hearing the sounds of my knee being operated on and viewing my insides on a monitor might not be the soundest choice I'd made. As Shakespeare wrote, "The better part of valor is discretion." In this case, it's the better part of pallor as well.

> As Shakespeare wrote, "The better part of valor is discretion." In this case, it's the better part of pallor as well.

I recognized my weaknesses and made a sensible choice based on those limitations. As runners, we're inclined to not set boundaries on ourselves, to consistently challenge our abilities, and to push the envelope. Those are all wonderful traits, but sometimes we need to recognize the reality of the situation. When you haven't trained sufficiently for a race, perhaps it's not the greatest plan to set overly aggressive minutes-per-mile pace. There's more than a solid likelihood you're going to end up looking like a piece of road kill in shorts and a singlet.

It's no different than it was choosing my event for high school track. I could have either gone with getting left in the dust in the 100-meter dash or, recognizing my limited natural sprinting ability, instead chosen the long-distance events to better my chances of winning. Sound strategy.

Similarly, if I acknowledge my limitations and know I'm likely to need an airsickness bag at the first sight of my medial collateral ligament on the video screen, well then, the best choice is to err on the side of caution. As in, unconsciousness can work quite well at times. Of course, as long as that's your conscious choice.

And, with me, it was. Now don't get me wrong. At times, it's obviously necessary to work on improving inherent weaknesses or limitations, but at other times it's necessary to recognize the reality of the moment. In recognizing my knee-viewing limitations, lights out equaled sights out.

Good choice.

Jack of No Trades, Master of Run

Learning on the Run Is Part of the Fun

CHAPTER 28

Lessons Learned, Lessons Spurned

Wacky wisdom gleaned from years on the run

Many of us are familiar with the saying that the definition of insanity is doing the same thing over and over and expecting different results. The origin of that saying has been attributed to everyone from Albert Einstein to Mark Twain to Benjamin Franklin. But I'm thinking the definition could best be attributed to a runner who has hit the marathon wall time and time again, has not learned from past mistakes, and is willing to do it over and over while expecting the outcome to be different. That rather thickheaded approach is a good reflection of the appropriateness of the title to this book and an accurate depiction of my experience in my first few marathon endeavors. I consistently abandoned all common sense while abruptly and firmly planting myself head first into the unforgiving wall. Each subsequent race felt as though my face were flattened a little further.

I would go out way too fast each marathon after determining within the first 600 yards that the best approach would be to immediately lower my goal pace significantly. Patience not only wasn't my virtue, it also wasn't even in my purview.

Each marathon experience was remarkably similar: I'd feel great early and run too fast the first half of the race, and then my pace would begin to slow. Somewhere between miles 18 and 21, I'd enter a hallucinatory fog and be greeted with the feeling that I was giving a piggyback ride to an obese rhinoceros as I painfully shuffled to the finish line.

Despite these gruesome experiences, it didn't stop me from doing it again and again, making the same mistake over and over. But I was an equal opportunity overadrenalized runner. I didn't limit myself to going out too fast only in the marathon distance. What fun would that have been?

> Somewhere between miles 18 and 21, I'd enter a hallucinatory fog and be greeted with the feeling that I was giving a piggyback ride to an obese rhinoceros as I painfully shuffled to the finish line.

My predilection for violating the cardinal pacing rule occurred in shorter races as well. My opening mile in the 10K would always be about 30 seconds faster than my final average mile pace. I also recall my first half marathon of many years ago and shooting for a pace slightly less than 6:00 per mile. To ask whether I got caught up in the excitement of the race is like asking whether Violet Beauregarde like gum. Ya think? I vividly remember hearing the seconds being called out at the first mile: "50, 53, 56." When I heard that, I concluded I was right on target at 5:56-mile pace. My heart skipped more than a few beats when the volunteer then bellowed out "five minutes" as I passed by. I was an entire minute faster than I should have been by the first mile! Not really a strong strategy. But I did subsequently learn pace patience. My improved race times were the proof in the pudding. More aptly, I was no longer the pacing goof in the pudding.

The concept of what I'd learned over my years of running came to mind recently when reading a book called *30 Lessons for Living*. The book offers wisdom from over 1,000 elderly people who were interviewed as part of the Legacy Project at Cornell University. The advice is based on what these people felt they did correctly and incorrectly during their lives. We would like to believe that with age comes wisdom, but as actor and comedian Tom Wilson said, "Sometimes age just shows up all by itself." But for the contributors to the book, age didn't show up without their having gained practical knowledge along the way. I figured if someone ever wanted to do a similar book with advice limited to running, then I'd be a decent source, because with my age comes tried-and-true running wisdom. Some things have worked, some things haven't, some mistakes, some retakes.

I've compiled a few running-related words of wisdom. Feel free to decide what to take to heart, what to take as not smart, and what to take to the race start:

- Running through an injury will be as successful as surfing through a tsunami.
- Beware of SSS, otherwise known as spaghetti surplus syndrome. One can experience an overload from carbo-loading and arrive at the starting line the next morning feeling like a bloated beached whale in an overly tight singlet.
- Vaseline is a magic elixir. It cures everything: blisters, chafing, windburn, and chapped lips. It also removes gum from hair and keeps your Halloween pumpkin from rotting. (Okay, the last two have nothing to do with running but are worthy attributes of petroleum jelly nonetheless.)
- Listen to your pain. It's really saying, "Hey, Nimrod! You keep going and this ends ugly."
- Failing to run training miles at goal pace and expecting to be able to hit that pace on race day is akin to having only hummed the song in your head that you're going to sing at an audition.
- A starting gun and race bib do not miraculously produce untapped speed. Running at the same modest pace every day equals running at the same modest pace during a race, which equals finishing in the same modest time.
- If you go out too fast, you'll come back too slow.

If you go out too fast, you'll come back too slow.

- Always listen to the little voice in your head telling you to just get out the door and run. That voice is perpetually brilliant.

- Take the steps necessary to prevent an injury, which will allow you to steer clear of missing running steps caused by the recovery from an avoidable injury.

- While running, acknowledge your presence when approaching a nonrunner from behind. It prevents a potential knee-jerk-reaction assault from an in-my-own-world-listening-to-my-iTunes startled pedestrian.

- All race courses are not created equal.

- Have a short memory of abysmal race performances and an elephant-like memory of the triumphant ones. And remember, no one but perhaps your significant other really cares how you did. Stay humble, my friend.

- Long runs can be tedious, trying, and time consuming. That's why they're called long.

- If you avoid running hills in training, it's fairly certain the race director won't let you avoid them during a race.

> Long runs can be tedious, trying, and time consuming. That's why they're called long.

- The old adage "You'll never know unless you try," is simple and accurate and may be difficult to follow. May as well try, though.

- If you aren't making mistakes in your running, then you're not doing anything. It's good to shake things up and see what may work for you.

- Go with quality over quantity or go with quantity over quality. But going with an excessive amount of anything equals a bad thing.

- If you up your weekly mileage to see how high you can go before physically breaking down, you will soon find out how high is too high. Better to know how high is almost too high. Otherwise you'll be laid low.

- It's sometimes as difficult to predict at the beginning of run how you'll feel during the middle of a run as it is to predict what song will be number 32 on Billboard's Top 100 in the year 2029.
- If you don't try to produce a kick at the end of a race, you'll subsequently kick yourself.
- You can run slow too much, run fast too much, hydrate too much, wear too much clothing, consume too much energy gel, run hills too much, and so on. Beware of the toos.
- Black toenails, blisters, and calluses can pretty much be avoided, but you'd miss displaying these badges of honor.
- Runners who don't look like runners will run faster than you. Runners who look like fast runners will run slower than you. You shouldn't look to run faster than other runners, like author William Faulkner said, "Don't bother just to be better than your contemporaries or predecessors. Try to be better than yourself." The other stuff then takes care of itself.
- Plastic sandwich bags are the panacea for cold hands and feet. Plastic trash bags are the panacea for prerace cold and postrace chills. Panacea is a nice word.
- A slow recovery run when you're whooped is much harder to accomplish than a strenuous fartlek workout when you're feeling good. Welcome the hard days.
- The world of running is not jerk proof.
- Sweat is the purifier of the soul.
- Take advantage of bad running days and take advantage of good running days. Take advantage of running.
- Polyester does get wet.
- If pain from injury goes away in the first mile, it doesn't mean it's gone for good.
- Sometimes race clocks don't tell the whole story. Your best race may be your worst time.
- And last: Running is simple. Don't complicate it.

CHAPTER
29

Who Can Leap Standing Water in a Single Bound?

The peculiar talents of Runnerman and Runnerwoman

Runners usually have their own particular running-related issue, which they're forced to deal with from time to time. Perhaps your Achilles' heel is that your Achilles tendinitis won't fully heal, or you're prone to foot blisters or to chafing in sundry areas, or you tend to experience lovely rib cage cramps after 20 miles. Maybe your issue is you have flat feet, or prerace insomnia prevents you from obtaining more than a grand total 57 minutes of fitful sleep. Or you may have an overactive bladder requiring knowledge of the location of all public restrooms within five miles of your house. I don't have any of these problems or even a profuse-sweating issue, but I certainly have my own issue.

Although there are a lot of phenomena I'd like to see in my lifetime from the Dead Sea to the Cave of Crystals, at present, the only phenomenon I've experienced is a condition I share with many others called Raynaud's phenomenon. That's my issue. Sounds impressive, but, for many like me who have a mild form of this condition, it's really an inconvenience. We're the ones running with mittens on even though the temperature is in the 50s, and in the winter we buy our running shoes half a size or more too big so we can accommodate the extra layering required to keep our toes warm.

Raynaud's phenomenon produces a constriction of the blood vessels mainly in the hands and toes, and the decreased blood supply produces discoloration and numbness. Emotional stress and cold are classic triggers of the disorder, so a bit of prerace anxiety and cooler temperatures can cause a doubly chilling whammy for me. In its milder form, Raynaud's is a nuisance given one has to plan accordingly to keep his or her digits warm at all times and avoid problems. Australian Aborigines have their three-dog night, when it is so cold they surround themselves with the warmth of three dogs. I've got my three-mitten morning during the peak of winter's chill wherein I've learned I can keep my fingers toasty with an initial layer of a plastic sandwich bag, followed by a fleece mitten and a pair of large heavy-duty, thoroughly insulated waterproof mittens on top. It might appear that I'm wearing huge sparring gloves, but my fingers are nice and warm, and a bonus is that cross-training is built in while my arms get a solid workout carrying the extra weight.

As with my personal solutions to difficulties caused by cooler temperature, runners develop their own abilities to successfully combat their particular running-related nemesis. This includes putting extra lubricant on chafing areas and men putting tape over their nipples to prevent painful irritation. Like the *Superman* television show's opening narration, my alter ego of Raynaud's Runnerman has evolved to the following:

> Warmer than a down blanket! More comfortable than sitting in a tepid sauna! Able to keep toes cozy with a few accessories! Yes, it's Raynaud's Runnerman who's learned how to have sweaty fingers in subzero temperatures and toasty toes in ankle-deep snow, and who, disguised as a mild-mannered winter runner, continues his pursuit of warmth, circulation, and the comfortably heated way!

Runnerman and Runnerwoman are also resourceful in not only combating their respective issue, but also in developing unique talents that nonrunners don't possess. Runnerman knows the exact number of minutes a large load of just-washed running clothes will take to fully dry. Runnerwoman can attach a running race chip to her shoelaces in 6.4 seconds, and Runnerman can name more muscles in his lower leg than he can name presidential cabinet positions. Runnerwoman can spread Shoe Goo on the heel of her shoe as delicately and efficiently as a concrete masonry expert.

Runnerman can pin a race number to his singlet in 14 seconds and have it positioned straighter than if he'd used a carpenter's ruler. Runnerwoman can efficiently grab a cup at a race aid station and quickly down the drink without breaking stride, and, more importantly, without drowning herself. Runnerman can effectively serve as a human pace chart through his talent of rapidly calculating the projected race time of any distance from 5K to 100 miles when supplied with the average mile pace. Runnerwoman can, without looking at her GPS watch, tell you the distance of a just-completed training run to within .16 miles, and Runnerman knows the exact lengths of all roads within 12 miles of his house. Runnerwoman knows the precise timing and quantity of a prerace meal to prevent her stomach from feeling like a lead balloon at the starting line, and Runnerman can quickly convert the kilometer speed limit signs in Canada.

We all have our running-related talent and we also have our way of dealing with personal nemeses. So you'll understand if you see me in the early summer wearing gloves on a morning run. Similarly, I'll understand if I see you playing amateur podiatrist and sterilizing a paper clip, and then delicately putting it into your toe to relieve the pressure of a black toenail. Whatever works.

Marc Davis, former U.S. Olympian in the steeplechase, said, "All it takes is all you got." Runners learn to do whatever it takes in training as well as to do whatever it takes to make other elements of their running go as smoothly as possible. And if that means walking backward down the stairs for the first week after a marathon because sore quadriceps are screaming and feel like silly putty, well a runner's got to do what a runner's go to do.

Phoning It In

Taking the talk test to a whole new level

When I'm running solo, I'd like to believe that I'm engaged in pensive activity. Communing with nature during the solitude of the early morning and sorting out the secrets of life, solving world problems, or outlining the next Pulitzer Prize–winning novel.

The reality is I may begin my run with a brief internal debate regarding U.S. economics, but I'm quickly moving on to not-so-scholarly ruminations. I'm often pondering life's less-than-critical questions such as can you decide that you're indecisive? Why are things typed up and written down? Is it an effective training method to periodically hold your breath as long as you can during a run? Why do we say an alarm clock is going off when it's on? My mind is a series of rapid segues with no rational connection involved.

Despite my fairly witless thoughts, I enjoy the solitude of running and am sufficiently entertained. When not focused on key issues like coming up with the synonym for thesaurus, the first half of my run often produces a list of things to do, and the second half is spent trying to remember just what those things were. Eleven-letter, memory-aiding acronyms are not uncommon by the end of a long run. Many times my run ends with my sprinting into the house, waving off conversation with my wife while scrambling for pen and paper as I repetitively mouth acronyms like ABSORLATION.

For the majority of my running career, I avoided bringing along forms of distraction or entertainment such as music or podcasts. Admittedly, I did dabble with audio books for a few runs. However, that was a recipe for failure given my inability to stay focused during a run on anything much beyond a mesmerizing five-word sentence. I quickly opted for the abridged versions but completely gave up upon learning there was no abridged version of the abridged version.

Being a music lover, I have in the more recent past taken advantage of the relative ease in which I can pipe my favorite songs into my sweaty ears during a run. Just me, my iPod shuffle, empty streets, and my jolting my neighbors awake by belting out a chorus from AC/DC's "You Shook Me all Night Long."

I've seen a lot over the years as far as what others choose to bring along for company or entertainment on a run, including the standard items, such as an infant (or two) in a running stroller or a dog or motivating music. But I've also seen the oddity of an elderly runner pushing his wife down the street in a wheelchair, as well as runners gliding along with what appears to be a five-course meal attached to their waist belt. I've also been amused by the lady "walking" her dog while she's driving her car. I've been privy to a man minus his skivvies: A naked guy on a bike rode by me in New York City at 5:00 a.m. yelling, "Top of the morning!"

Every now and then I do witness things, like the birthday suit bicyclist, that cause me to break stride and do a running double take. A few years back while I was running along the gorgeous and bucolic paths of a local state park with the rising sun reflecting off a still lake, I saw a runner coming up over the crest of the hill ahead. At first I couldn't believe my eyes, or my ears. Couldn't be. Wouldn't be. Shouldn't be. Ah, but it was.

> **Just me, my iPod shuffle, empty streets, and my jolting my neighbors awake by belting out a chorus from AC/DC's "You Shook Me all Night Long."**

The Lord of the Rings was approaching, but I don't mean someone resembling the Witch-king of Angmar. I mean rings, as in a phone call.

There he was, a man answering the cell phone he was carrying (his ring tone the less-than-idyllic sound of MC Hammer's "U Can't Touch This"). Mr. Fartlek Fiber Optics with the truly mobile phone was bringing new meaning to the term long-distance communication.

Now, I understand there may be a need to stay connected from time to time and be in touch through a cell phone regarding an emergency or whatever. However, I encountered him on a trail many miles from the nearest parking lot, and his ear-splitting conversation clearly was not with 911 but with a more-than-jovial friend on the other end of the line.

His thunderous voice and overenthusiastic laughter were in direct contrast to my harmonious rendezvous with nature. As squirrels scattered for the park's higher ground and terrified ducks rapidly exited the lake, it would have been rhetorical should he have voiced the slogan "Can you hear me now?" Lord Alfred Tennyson wrote, "O hark. O Hear! How thin and clear." This was more "The park. O dear! The din, I sneer!"

As I ran by I gave him a disdainful look and sarcastically said, "Really?" Through subsequent years I still remain irked by Mr. Ringing Runner, but I admit to seeing the emergence of more running and cell phone use. I've witnessed cell phones immediately materializing from the waistbands of runners as they cross a finish line. I've also seen pictures being taken on a cell phone right before the starting gun goes off and undoubtedly then uploaded to Twitter, with 23 reply tweets posted before the runner crosses the starting line. In more ways than one, the times they are a changing.

I suppose, on further reflection, that I shouldn't be so hard on peripatetic phone callers. At least they're out running rather than perfecting their touch-tone mobility abilities or texting-in-motion talents through a more sedentary position. Perhaps I need to simply accept things a bit more. As Roman politician Cicero once said, "To each his own."

I suppose it could be rephrased simply "To each his phone."

CHAPTER 31

Fashionable Fartleks

Wick me away!

Ask a runner what's the greatest running-related innovation to come along and you'll get many answers: heart rate monitor, fuel belt, GPS watch, protection from nipple chafing, encapsulated compression sport bras. And, of course we can't dismiss the tasty, energizing, vitamin-filled, caffeinated, and candy-like fueling products.

However, I reached a different conclusion recently as I came back from a cold, snowy, winter run. I unzipped my breathable, reflective, vented, waterproof, and windproof jacket and then removed my insulating fleece layer and perspiration-wicking base layer and, last, my synthetic tights. I couldn't help but hearken back to the cotton running clothing of yesteryear. Long gone are the days of cumbersome sweats where perspiration, freezing rain, and dropping temperatures could transform my top into a rock-solid icy sweatshirt, which I'd have to literally shatter upon arriving home in order to get it over my head. I gave new meaning to the term ice chest. The only good thing was that when it hailed, I could do my best super hero imitation because my hardened top served as an indestructible shield against the pounding baseball-sized projectiles of frozen rain. Captain America of the winter running world!

Admittedly, the comfort of cotton has a large place in my non-running wardrobe, although referencing it as a wardrobe is a bit of hyperbole. My collection of clothes includes less-than-fashionable

T-shirts with expressions such as "Obsessed is a word lazy people use to describe the dedicated," and "90% of running is half mental." Cotton is great for many things, but its downfall in the running arena is its ability to absorb and retain. Those two traits might be great for speed-reading but not so good during a summer run with a high heat index. It's then that a running top can easily become permanently suctioned to one's torso.

My vote for best running-related innovation? Is there anything better than a fiber-forming substance with a long-chain synthetic polymer composed of at least 85 percent by weight of an ester of dihydric alcohol and terephthalic acid that is derived from polyethylene terephthalate? Okay, I admit to having absolutely no clue what that definition means because I was lost at fiber-forming. All

> Those two traits might be great for speed-reading but not so good during a summer run with a high heat index. It's then that a running top can easily become permanently suctioned to one's torso.

that I retained from chemistry class is the pivotal knowledge that Bunsen burners are hot, test tubes shatter rather easily if dropped, and always team up with a lab partner who actually listened to the teacher's instructions. I do know, though, that my favorite running-related innovation goes by the more common name of polyester. But don't ask me how it functions. It's like with a Teflon-coated pan: I don't know how it works or why it works, only that it does work. And polyester works.

One of the many attractions of polyester is that it is hydrophobic, which I'm certainly not, but some of my best shirts are. Being water repellant, polyester keeps us comfortable by wicking perspiration away from the skin. It possesses incredibly quick drying capabilities. It usually becomes devoid of moisture during the 2.46 seconds it takes me to move my clothes from the washer to the dryer. It graciously keeps us cooler in the summer and warmer in the winter. It's like the old joke where a not-so-astute person believes that the greatest invention is the thermos because it keeps its contents either hot or cold. The person is perplexed and asks, "How does it know?" Hey, polyester knows.

Polyester running apparel has also brought us out of the dark ages of gray drawstring sweat pants. We've evolved from simply entering the wicking world and moved even further into today's synthetic outfits that are neon colored, antibacterial, antimildew, wrinkle free, seamless, resilient, antichafing, nonshrinking, and easily washable and that protect us from ultraviolet rays and retain their color. Phew. And you thought your new polyester shirt simply looked good with your green shorts!

We've gone from not sticking out because of our clothing to being running fashion statements in our vibrant polyester running clothing that addresses all body parts from neck gaiters to compression socks. The fact is I have no fashion sense. More like fashion nonsense. It's not that I'm color blind and believe my running attire always matches; it's more that I've never really given clothing colors a whole lot of thought. Perhaps this stems from so many years of simply snatching my running gear from my drawers in the dark like a giant closet grab-bag game. I only knew what I had on if the sun rose during my run and I could see my clothing for the first time. Sure I'd know if I had short or long sleeves or shorts or tights, but color? No clue. No hue.

Polyester clothing evolution has provided us with specialized apparel to address every appendage and exposed area of our epidermis. It has also taken the guesswork out of what to wear in response to the elements. Not sure whether

> I only knew what I had on if the sun rose during my run and I could see my clothing for the first time. Sure I'd know if I had short or long sleeves or shorts or tights, but color? No clue. No hue.

a singlet is enough? Then throw on some thermal, compression arm sleeves, and roll them down or off if it gets too warm. Not entirely certain whether a thermal hat is necessary? Then go with a lightweight, contoured skull cap or a moisture-wicking, chill-resistant headband or even a winter cap with fleece ear flaps for that attractive beagle look. Undecided on the need for mittens, then break out that polyester top with thumb holes in the extended sleeves in case your fingers get cold. We're able to leave nothing to chance and nothing for thought as we've removed the whether from the weather.

Word is that our clothing will soon include the ability to generate electricity through kinetic energy produced by our body's movement and captured by our garments. It is thought that enough energy would be generated to power personal devices like music players.

Now if I could just get my polyester singlet to give my enervated body enough of a charge to get up a long hill at mile 20, then we'd be talking! Synthesize that!

PART

IX

Enjoying the View on the Competitive Drive

Keeping Perspective Is Good, but Elusive

To Thine Own Self Be You

There are multiple paths to the mountaintop. The key is finding your itinerary

One of my most unanticipated race performances occurred years ago when my family and I visited relatives in southern California over the Fourth of July weekend. We landed very late Friday night and spent 13 not-so-tranquil hours at congested Disneyland on Saturday, and in the epitome of a "What was I thinking?" moment, I entered a 10K race on Sunday morning.

I was fairly certain no training books recommended the pre-race strategy of inducing significant jet lag, walking mega miles in an amusement park in sweltering heat the day before, and then topping everything off with a day-before-the-race smorgasbord of cotton candy, cinnamon rolls, fried green tomato sandwich, a loaded burrito, onion rings, chocolate bread pudding, and a milkshake. For good measure, grab a loaded funnel cake right before exiting the park, toss in a miserable night's sleep, don't taper at all, and then take a wrong turn to the race, limiting warm-up time to about 43 seconds. All in all it isn't exactly the recipe for a great 10K performance, let alone a comfortable 50-yard walk.

With my body saying I should have fueled up with a quadruple espresso, I stood at the starting line prepared for an onerous race and a meager time. Where was the lovely Tinkerbell from the day before with her magical pixie dust when I needed her most?

Surprisingly, though, once the starting gun went off, I felt amazingly spry and wound up running a great race. In subsequent races, I stopped just short of incor-

> For good measure grab a loaded funnel cake right before exiting the park, toss in a miserable night's sleep, don't taper at all, and then take a wrong turn to the race, limiting warm-up time to about 43 seconds.

porating a Disneyland diet or simulated jet lag into my prerace strategy. However, the experience reinforced my view that sometimes you can't determine what factored into your running performance, and perhaps a couple of pounds of cotton candy the day before had worked for me.

I've been unpleasantly surprised the other way as well. There've been times when I'm primed, rested, and ready for a speedy training run. Not so fast, Twinkle Toes. One mile in and it was back to the drawing board as I quickly downgraded a planned fartlek workout to a very slow and easy run to ultimately calculating how long it would take to jog straight back home!

Along these lines, I'm often reminded of the wisdom of the late, great running philosopher George Sheehan who said, "We are each an experiment of one." What works for you may not work for me. Heck, what works for me today may not work for me tomorrow.

The newest training advice may propel you to a PR and may catapult me to the back of the pack. Figuring out what works best for you is indeed the ongoing experiment of one.

Many examples exist of successful runners who have had rather unique approaches to training. Emil Zatopek (gold medal winner in 5,000 meters, 10,000 meters, and the marathon at the 1952 Olympics) used to sometimes train in army boots while running with his wife (a gold medal javelin thrower) on his shoulders! I'm thinking it's a pretty sure bet my wife isn't getting up extra early in the morning so I can parade her around the neighborhood on my back.

Different training approaches are no more apparent than with the obsession many runners have with an average weekly-mileage

I'm often reminded of the wisdom of the late, great running philosopher George Sheehan who said, "We are each an experiment of one." What works for you may not work for me. Heck, what works for me today may not work for me tomorrow.

total. Japanese runner Toshihiko Seko (winner of the famous Fukuoka marathon four times and the Boston Marathon twice) trained a marathon per day (182 miles per week), while Greg Meyer, the last American to win the Boston Marathon, achieved his success at a lower number of about 100 miles per week. Experiments of one.

When I turned 50, I whimsically figured what better time to determine exactly how many miles per week I could achieve before physically beginning to break down. Kind of like the high-performance centrifuge testing of a NASA astronaut to see how much gravitational force could be withstood before losing consciousness. Of course, the astronauts had a much nobler goal of serving their country in the space race. My more purposeless challenge would not be backed up by the soundest training methods, but it would be cheaper than traditional reactions to a midlife crisis, such as buying a sports car.

I'd read that former Olympic marathon champion Joan Benoit Samuelson (three years my senior) was hitting nearly 80 miles per week at 50, and masters 5K champ and runner extraordinaire, Pete Magill, was hitting 90 miles per week. Most significantly, octogenarian Ed Whitlock, during marathon training, ran up to three hours every day around a short loop in a cemetery (shunning stretching as well as speed work). At age 80 he was still cranking out world record after world record from the marathon (3:25:43) to the 1,500 meters. When I hit 80, I'd just hope to find my shoes each morning!

If they could run such high mileage, then so could I! So what if 80 miles per week was the upper end of my mileage back in my heyday (which was waaaay back). So what if I'd run from injury to injury the last few years? Don't bother me with such sensible questions.

> I ventured up my own experimental mileage ladder and got past 60, 65, and 70 and did a few 73 weeks. I was feeling great with no pains and racing strong. But as I pushed onward to the magical 75, injury free suddenly became "Woe is me."

I ventured up my own experimental mileage ladder and got past 60, 65, and 70 and did a few 73 weeks. I was feeling great with no pains and racing strong. But as I pushed onward to the magical 75, injury free suddenly became "Woe is me."

I instantly broke down like an old jalopy being pushed to 100 miles per hour causing its parts to suddenly fall apart en masse. Although the astronaut's body provided signals when the g-force during the centrifuge testing was getting too high, I had no such signs of impending doom. Unannounced and abruptly, the Big Three P trifecta of injury arrived, otherwise known as piriformis syndrome, plantar fasciitis, and patellar tendinitis. In my experiment of one, I was now over and done.

I eventually healed, experimented further, and adopted a more palatable weekly mileage total. An amount more consistent with record-setting Linda Somers Smith, who downsized her average weekly mileage to 50 miles per week (with solid speed work plus cross-training) and churned out a 1:13:32 half marathon and a 2:36:33 marathon at 49 years old.

We are indeed all different. Don't bother telling Yoshihisa Hosaka of Japan about the benefits of the well-accepted hard-day, easy-day training approach. Most masters runners modify that approach even further by having a hard day, then an easy day, then a very, very easy day, then maybe a day-off day. Hosaka took the completely opposite approach. He did the same very hard workout every day and cranked out marathon times of 2:32:27 at 50 (and a 2:36:30 at 60). He averaged nearly 20 miles per day, and much of that was done at marathon pace or faster (and through extremely detailed interval training). A training approach that would require even most 30-year-olds to taper before attempting even one day of this regimen. And at twice that age, Hosaka was cruising quite nicely, doing it daily. His approach didn't just fly in the face of conventional wisdom, it also soared way above it.

On the other side of the starting line is the simplistic approach of Jack Foster, who at age 40, placed eighth in the Olympic marathon and at 41 set a world masters marathon mark of 2:11:18 that lasted 16 years. His philosophy was neatly summed up with "I don't train; never have. I don't think of running as training. I just go out and run each day, and let the racing take care of itself." All of which made Foster the king of laid back, but which also put him around the front of the elite pack.

The bottom line is we are all, indeed, experiments of one, and a single training approach won't fit everyone. No matter whether it's Jeff Galloway's run-walk-run approach, the quick bursts of high-intensity sprint interval training (SIT), shortened tapers, or the choice to run in shoes versus barefoot, it all comes down to what works best for you.

So go ahead and tinker and be a mad scientist, a fad scientist, even at times a bad scientist in your own experiment of one. As for me, I'll always recall that successful post-Disneyland race.

So, please feel free to pass me more of that cotton candy and don't hold back on the funnel cake either. I'm going for broke.

Climb Every Mountain or at Least a Small Mound Now and Then

Go with the flow and redefine slow

I grew up in a pretty competitive household and was raised on the philosophy of veteran tennis great Martina Navratilova, who said, "Whoever said, 'It's not whether you win or lose that counts,' probably lost." I'm not sure my most admirable trait as a youngster was wanting to obliterate my grandmother in gin rummy. But I didn't care and often had to restrain myself from doing a victory dance around her kitchen table while waving my cards in the air.

Years later, I recall my father playing my 5-year-old son in the Connect Four board game. After losing rather handily, my father was mortified and quickly exited our home. He then purchased his own game, devised strategies, and practiced for hours against my mother. He entered our home early one morning with his game face on and saying nothing more than, "Where is he?" When I told him his grandson was at kindergarten (subtly reminding my dad that his opponent was still learning his ABCs), my father replied that he'd wait. I shook my head and politely escorted him out. His behavior confirmed where some of my not-so-laudable competitive inclinations derived from. I'm convinced that if I had allowed them to play again and my father had won, he'd probably have lightly heckled his grandson with "Who's King Connect Four now, little man? Better bring your A game next time!"

Over time, my competitive zeal greatly diminished against anyone other than myself. My wife, whose competitive athletic fires never even rose to the smoldering stage, was most responsible for causing those changes in me. When our children arrived, she helped me refrain from continuously quoting former New York Jets football coach Herm Edwards, who famously said with maniacal eyes and a stern voice, "You play to win the game!" I recall staring across the ping-pong table at my 8-year-old son, convincing myself that it would not be a notch in my belt to obliterate someone half my size and who had, 20 minutes earlier, begun playing the game for the first time. I also refrained from sulking after my 13-year-old daughter beat me at Words With Friends and am proud to say I didn't keep her up well past midnight with rematch after rematch, trying for that critical, but elusive, victory.

It was more difficult, though, to remove Coach Lombardi's "Winning is the only thing" philosophy from my running, and not just with races but also in everyday training. I was pathetic enough to allow a weekend to be ruined by not only a poor race performance but also by a slower than normal workout. Don't get me wrong; I was addicted to the pure joy

> I recall staring across the ping-pong table at my 8-year-old son, convincing myself that it would not be a notch in my belt to obliterate someone half my size and who had, 20 minutes earlier, begun playing the game for the first time.

of running and all it brought to my life, but competitive over-drive with myself often took control. I was that runner whose nerves caused an inability to sleep the night before a race because I consistently failed to appreciate that the race was inconsequential in the grand scheme of life. For an out-of-town race, I was most interested in finding a hotel with a picturesque ceiling to stare at and plenty of cable channels to click through at 3:00 a.m. The latter was warranted because many years ago on a pre-marathon night, the channel selection in my hotel room was pretty much limited to a repetitive loop of Suzanne Somers' ThighMaster infomercial. The next morning, I couldn't get "Squeeze your way to a shapely figure," out of my head for the entire race!

I do recall the only time my prerace persona of Captain Anxiety allowed a hint of a relaxed smile. It was years ago when I was running the Bermuda Marathon with Leukemia Team in Training. In all my marathons up to that point I'd broken three hours, but with a lack of sufficient long runs coming into the race, I'd conceded that goal was unlikely. I tried to convince myself to relax and just have fun, that the run was for a good cause, and so on. Unfortunately, my mindset changed into personal battle mode within the first 53 yards. Insanity prevailed, and, although I kept my streak alive, I barely kept myself alive. I bonked and was bonkers at the same time with my abnormal competitive intensity. It wasn't pretty. I should have followed the running proverb that "Pride goes before a crawl."

However, in later years, something finally occurred that allowed me to mollify my less-than-admirable competitive behavior: I got slow. I don't mean a three-toed sloth on tranquilizers slow, but slower than I'd ever been. I'd fought the good fight to keep Father Time from coming in through the front door, but the bearded guy with the robe, scythe, and hourglass was very sneaky. He'd somehow made his way to my closet and more specifically into my running shoes. And on some runs it felt like I was carrying him on my back.

I eventually accepted the fact I'd never again set a personal record unless a course was mismeasured. But without the same competitive fire in my belly, would I run just to prevent a tire around my belly?

The fact is I would always run because of the sheer joy it brought me, but I learned I could retune things a bit and maintain a healthy competition with myself in various ways. Competing to go for a run each day, even when life or Mother Nature was getting in the way, to continue the fight to come back from injuries, to run hard a couple times a week to the point of near exhaustion not because of the quest for a PR but for the satisfaction of a solid effort. I learned not to be so hard on myself, and I kept climbing the proverbial mountain, but I also accepted that some days climbing up a small mound would be just fine.

> I'd fought the good fight to keep Father Time from coming in through the front door, but the bearded guy with the robe, scythe and hourglass was very sneaky. He'd somehow made his way to my closet and more specifically into my running shoes.

I also came across this poem, which I keep on my desk to provide a constant reminder that the pleasurable act of running is what it is all about. A 19-year-old Scottish Army officer, Charles Hamilton Sorley, wrote the poem during World War I.

The Song of the Ungirt Runners

We swing ungirded hips,
And lightened are our eyes,
The rain is on our lips,
We do not run for prize.
We know not whom we trust
Nor whitherward we fare,
But we run because we must

Through the great wide air.
The waters of the seas
Are troubled as by storm.
The tempest strips the trees
And does not leave them warm.
Does the tearing tempest pause?
Do the tree-tops ask it why?
So we run without a cause
'Neath the big bare sky.

The rain is on our lips,
We do not run for prize.
But the storm the water whips
And the wave howls to the skies.
The winds arise and strike it
And scatter it like sand,
And we run because we like it
Through the broad bright land.

I can still train and race with a healthy measure of personal competition and know that the gratification derived from the feat of a hard run greatly outweighs the disappointment of a slower-than-normal result. More importantly, I know that when the time comes that I have a grandson, I can accept his beating me in a competitive game of Connect Four. Although I may tell my wife I let the little guy win.

I didn't say I was completely cured.

Just Lose, Baby!

There is joy in Mudville

Foreign languages and science classes weren't my forte in school. I recall trying to combine the two in the effort to convince my academic counselor that my chemistry class should also fulfill my foreign language requirement because it was all Greek to me. No such *suerte*. I remember little from my exposure to German beyond *Gesundheit* and one other word. It's this latter word that has come to mind lately given some runners' comments regarding other runners. The word is *Schadenfreude*, which translates roughly to joy derived from someone else's misfortune. In the language of the running world, this was not the famous training line of "No pain, no gain." This was more "Your pain. My gain."

If misery loves company, then schadenfreude is more akin to company that loves misery. Not their misery, though. Yours! If people with a good dose of schadenfreude had been in Mudville, then there would have instead been joyous pandemonium when mighty Casey struck out!

Now, indeed, a nice sense of camaraderie exists within the running world, a common bond among runners given the commitment involved in training and participating in long-distance events. The sportsmanship of extending a congratulatory hand or engaging in a hug with a competitor who has just done well is consistently seen on the elite side as well as among the more recreational runners. But I learned two things when I began perusing message boards on various running-related websites. First, I learned that people are eager to ask for incongruous advice of readers who most likely have no knowledge of the off-topic query posed. It's not unusual to find someone actually asking a group of runners a nonrunning question to the tune of "I have a non-qualified variable deferred annuity with a pre-TEFRA cost basis of $10,000 that was purchased via a 1035 exchange; can someone explain the tax implications to my secondary beneficiaries and also by donating it to a 501(c)(3)?" You'd actually find respondents such as non-tax-attorney Plumber Earl, a runner from Biloxi, attempting to take a swing at answering that one.

> If misery loves company, then schadenfreude is more akin to company that loves misery. Not their misery, though. Yours! If people with a good dose of schadenfreude had been in Mudville, then there would have instead been joyous pandemonium when mighty Casey struck out!

Some of the running-related queries also raise the question of "Why are you asking that?" Such as "I can move my knee cap almost completely to the back of my leg and can't walk without incredible pain; would getting it checked out by a doctor be a good idea?" Ya think?

The second thing I learned is that some runners seemed to revel in the failure of other runners. They were full of schadenfreude. The posts weren't limited to the more acceptable criticism toward pompous and boasting athletes who may have earned their just desserts. Instead, the message boards resembled a schadenfreude open season on elite runners with no closing date in site.

This was readily evident in the posts regarding Ryan Hall. Hall is the American record holder in the marathon and half marathon, a two-time Olympian, and a top-three finisher at the Boston Marathon and is married to his college sweetheart, runner Sara Hall, with whom he operates a charitable foundation aimed at fighting global poverty. He also happens to be eminently likeable. Not exactly an object of derision. But in reading some of the message boards, you'd think in Hall's spare time he goes around telling as many young children as possible that there's no Santa Claus!

When Hall elected to split from his coach and train himself, he was completely vilified. Many predicted (and seemingly hoped) that his 2011 Boston Marathon would be an abysmal failure. When he had a bad outing at the New York City Half Marathon a month before Boston, many posters reveled in his failure. However, at Boston, Hall ran the fastest marathon for an American (2:04:58) and finished fourth. Since there was an inability to bask in the glow of schadenfreude, many posters tried to get some satisfaction in claiming Hall hadn't really run that well given that there was a strong tailwind. Last I knew, high winds didn't possess the ability to affect one runner alone out of 25,000-plus racers. Even if every participant had a jetpack, if you finished fourth overall at Boston, well, you had a pretty darn good race.

I try to shy away from feelings of schadenfreude but admit to being into running karma. Such as, if I'm out of commission because of an injury and have to hear Mr. Runner ad Nauseam tell me how his running is going so wonderfully, how magically euphoric his recent long run was, how not running must really eat away at me, and how he never, ever, ever gets injured! Of course, his willingness to state the latter can soon become the kiss of plantar fasciitis. I don't go so far as to secretly wish that his Achilles tendon ruptures in the first step he takes after his obnoxious monologue. But if at some point he's required to briefly join me on the injured list, I do get a slight bit of satisfaction in that bit of running karmic payback.

> Last I knew, high winds didn't possess the ability to affect one runner alone out of 25,000-plus racers. Even if every participant had his or her own jetpack, if you finished fourth overall at Boston, well, you had a pretty darn good race.

However, some posters on these message boards take schadenfreude to a whole new level. As with their take on Hall, these posters possess not only a high dose of pleasure in another's misfortune, but they also engage in what I refer to as pre-schadenfreude. They derive joy in simply predicting (and hoping) that a particular elite runner will be an epic failure at an upcoming major race. If the runner of their derision subsequently fails, these message board writers received even more jubilation. Being able to obtain both pre- and postrace joy, through their negative thoughts, enables them to accomplish the often elusive double schadenfreude!

It would be nice if these posters could display a bit more *mudita*, which is a Buddhist term for sympathetic joy in the happiness of another. In a strange way, one could actually get the best of both words. My conclusion actually materialized while ruminating during a nice 10-mile run. What I concluded was that through mudita, one could gain joy in the happiness of runners who'd achieved great performances. Conversely, a runner's failure in a major race would enable those Negative Nancy–types to obtain pleasure through schadenfreude. Combining the two, one could experience vicarious joy (mudita) by witnessing the pleasure the negative posters experienced (schadenfreude) when a runner monumentally failed. A no-lose, running-based, reverse catch-22! Perhaps it now goes without saying, my mind sometimes produces peculiar concepts during a run.

Or then again, maybe it's better not to deal with foreign words regarding how we should react toward fellow runners other than esprit de corps and camaraderie. It's best to simply encourage and cheer, enjoy the success of others, and build them back up after failure. We're all in this together.

Comrades-in-bonking!

Faster Finishing Counterparts

Setting the pace for the race within a race

It all started with Brandi Chaseton. No need to rack your brains trying to figure out whether she was the soccer player who scored the game-winning penalty kick for the United States in the 1999 Women's World Cup and then engaged in jersey-waving and sport-bra-baring celebration (that was Brandi Chastain) or the Washington-born singer of the popular "The Story" (that was Brandi Carlile). My Brandi is slightly less famous, although she plays a significant role in my life, even if she doesn't know it.

Brandi was one of the integral pieces that contributed to my getting on board the exhilarating road of competitive running. It goes all the way back to my fourth-grade field day, back to an age when boys raced against girls in the same event. Mano a womano! Now, some would say my running career pretty much peaked about the time I learned long division, as up to that point I'd been the sprinting sensation of the elementary school crowd. I was a virtual Usain Bolt of the playground and the fabulously fast 50-yard dash champion for four years running. Literally. But that was B.C. Before Chaseton.

That spring, new-to-our-school Brandi left me in the dust and in a distant second-place finish in the 50-yard dash. Girls had whooped me in everything, including spelling bees and math quiz bowls, but that was the first time one had kicked my butt in a race. I wasn't exactly the poster child for gracious losers. After my defeat, I protested that Brandi had false started. When that was met with deaf ears, I went with the premise that transfer students needed to sit out a year before gaining their field day eligibility! I followed that up with the request that the teachers demand to see her birth certificate! I possessed only a slight bit of sanity but was able to stop short of embarrassing myself further by demanding she produce a urine specimen.

Despite my protests, her victory stood and I was forced to decide over the next year whether I'd feign injury come fifth-grade field day, limit myself to the softball toss, or lace up my P.F. Flyers a little tighter and regain my champion status in the 50-yard dash. I chose the latter, but much to my dismay, my female nemesis opted for the shuttle run and long jump and bypassed the 50. *How dare she,* I thought! Apparently, Brandi had no clue of the competitive battle that had been raging in my prepubescent brain for 364 days. She couldn't do that! Where was my retribution! Where was the integrity of providing a rematch to the vanquished champion? Alas, it wasn't to be found on the dirt field behind the gym where I was left to claim a rather hollow fifth-grade victory.

> Girls had whooped me in everything, including spelling bees and math quiz bowls, but that was the first time one had kicked my butt in a race. I wasn't exactly the poster child for gracious losers.

By middle school I didn't have to worry about speedy Brandi and other girls blazing ahead of me because boys and girls were placed into separate events and never the twain shall (track) meet. Thus, I never had to deal at the same time with both teenage acne and losing to some local high school mile female phenomenon. However, after high school, I started participating in more road races, and the Brandi Chasetons of the world were again perched alongside me at the starting line. Ready, willing, and able to whoop me.

Now, don't get me wrong. I knew there were tons of women way, way faster than me. But it just so happened that in many of the more competitive races I participated in, my finishing time was usually in the vicinity of the winning female finisher. Knowing this, I found myself in the general area of the faster female runners and recognized that if I could pull ahead of them at the end, I'd have likely run a good

> Apparently, Brandi had no clue of the competitive battle that had been raging in my prepubescent brain for 364 days. She couldn't do that! Where was my retribution! Where was the integrity of providing a rematch to the vanquished champion?

race. Now, trust me. This was in no way, shape, or form a sexist thing. Rather, this was simply a measuring tool for my race performance rather than a reflection whatsoever of the view that I shouldn't be beaten by a woman. I quite distinctly learned that lesson early on from lightning bolt Brandi. This competitive thing could have easily been with the 20- to 24-year-old male division if that's who I was usually finishing along side of.

But as the years marched on, and I remained only slightly more mature than a 9-year-old, I had to begin a bit of rationalizing. For a long time, my record was pretty good and I could still stay ahead of my competitive female counterparts. However, as increasing age produced slower times, losses to the first-place woman began to enter the picture. I had my share of built-in excuses for whomever beat me, male or female or whatever, but I became more creative on my excuse meter with my gender-based competition. Much to the dismay of the speedy women runners in my self-imposed race within a race, I often engaged in a little postrace interrogation. I needed to determine whether they fell within my new exceptions: They, at one time or another, had a college cross country scholarship or they tapered for this race and I didn't.

Now, as I continue to get older (and not much more mature), and faster women continue to defeat me, I know I've got to become even more innovative. Perhaps the she's got to be nearly half my age exception.

Only time and many more Brandis will tell.

I needed to determine whether they fell within my new exceptions: They, at one time or another, had a college cross country scholarship or they tapered for this race and I didn't.

X

The Legs Have It! Don't Be Defeeted

Figuring Out What Will Keep You on the Streets

CHAPTER 36

May the Stick Be With You!

The magic wand to the land of self-massage

I'm a sucker for an infomercial touting the latest product that I can't live without. I was one of the first on my block to score with the original Veg-O-Matic. (It slices! It dices! It makes julienne fries!) I don't even fish, but still I took the bait from the commercial for the Pocket Fisherman. I couldn't pass it up after the entreating line from the pitchman "It's the biggest fishing invention since the hook!"

It's not that these products aren't useful. It's just that after my impulsive purchase, I find that I don't use them enough. I've got a Snuggie I've barely touched and a GT Xpress 101 grill that collects dust, and how could I ever forget the limited use I got out of the Perfect Situp or the Yoshi Blade.

My impulsive purchasing is not a whole lot different when it comes to running-related products. I'm definitely the one those small ads in the back of the running magazines target. My closet floor is littered with running-related things that I never needed or used. Headlamps? My only non-daylight runs occur on the remarkably well-lit roads of my neighborhood. Nipple protectors? I may chafe but never there. Toe caps? I still don't know what I got those for. Unbreakable shoelaces? My laces never broke before, so I don't know why I was concerned. Running greeting cards? Never sent them. Race number belt? I prefer safety pins and shirt. Pace bands? I am way too compulsive to not have memorized my splits before the race.

But there was, indeed, one useful product among all those items I'd bought. A few years ago I'd been repeatedly affected by pulled hamstring muscles and pulled calf muscles. This dastardly duo consistently conspired to make my running life miserable by first teasing me with their absence from my life, only to reappear and drop me back in the land of injury. I tried many remedies to fix the problem, but none of them provided consistent relief.

However, everything changed after a run in which I'd pulled a muscle and was lying on my bedroom floor, banging my fists with frustration. By happenstance, I saw something under my bed. There among running magazines from the late 1980s, a worn-out original pair of now retro New Balance 574s, and a legion of single stray running socks was something that resembled a rolling pin from my kitchen.

As I pulled it out, I couldn't recall what I'd purchased it for, but things slowly came back to me. It was The Stick, which I'd bought many years ago. It had only collected dust since. I should have appreciated that most things whose name begins with the word "The" are usually fairly impressive. Elvis was The King, John Wayne was The Duke, Bruce Springsteen is The Boss, and we had Babe Ruth as The Bambino. And then, there was The Stick.

I reacquainted myself with The Stick by first perusing the product's website. It was billed as a flexible tool made from "space age plastic" (although the space age was over 50 years ago, it still sounded impressive) with the critical component being the rolling spindles along the center rod. The latter were designed to provide a type of self-massage with maximum compression of the muscle, "turning non-compliant muscle into compliant muscle via stripping massage and diffusing trigger points." I wasn't completely sure what all that meant, but I was game to take plastic rotating spindles to my fibrous tissue, and, lo and behold, it was music to my muscles.

It wasn't as though after one round I trotted back out the door for a speedy pain-free 10 miler. But obsessively consistent use had me back on the roads and injury free from muscle pulls. I'd found euphoria in my magical wand of synthetic spindles!

They say there's not much worse than a reformed smoker and their annoying predilection for dispensing the how, why, and what regarding their ability to have quit. I became that guy. I became a walking, talking infomercial for The Stick! I was willing to tell, ad nauseam, anyone within earshot (and some well beyond) about the wonders of the powerful plastic instrument. I'd spout off to anyone I saw running and even told nonrunners if I saw anyone limping or even walking slowly. In line at the grocery store, the post office, the movies, there were no boundaries to my insatiable desire to spread the gospel of The Stick to any and all who would listen. Okay, in all honesty, listening was not a requirement. I'd impart the virtues of The Stick to uninterested strangers, friends, mailmen, and animals. I was the guy with the shtick for The Stick.

I'd use The Stick anywhere at anytime. I had one in my car, computer bag, garage, office, shower, and backyard. One couldn't be more than five yards from The Stick at any place in our house. My wife was fairly tolerant and knew an injured runner husband was way more difficult to handle than matching the color of our furniture with the yellow, white, and blue of The Stick.

As I remained free from muscle pulls and slightly over-the-top enamored with the wonders of The Stick, I confessed to wondering whether it might be effective in other ways. Like rolling the spindles across a receding hairline to induce hair growth or delicately massaging the nasal passages to cure the common cold. Dislodging kidney stones? You never know.

Although The Stick comes in various sizes and lengths, including The Travel Stick, I'm convinced they need one that runners can carry during a run and whip out at the first sign of muscle discomfort or fatigue. How convenient would it be in a marathon relay or ultra relay for a runner to also use this Stick as the actual race baton? The Multi-Purpose Stick.

Given my relentless preaching, it's common for me to see someone in my neighborhood running along and yelling out to me, "Got The Stick, Bob! Legs feel great! Thanks for the advice!"

Although I'm admittedly maniacal and compulsively persistent in touting its benefits to others, with my legion of converts The Stick has made me The Man. In a good way.

I think.

Not Fully Baring My Sole

Less is more in more ways than one

Many runners like me have felt toward the end of a race as though we've hit not just one wall, but a series of walls that resembles repetitive dominoes falling down upon us. As we agonizingly struggle forward and internally question our sanity, we often negotiate a runner's version of a Faustian bargain. In our glycogen deprived state, we pledge to no one in particular that in return for allowing us to finish alive and in one piece, we will never go out too fast again, do more goal-pace training runs, stretch for more than 43 seconds a day, and refrain from squeezing in that last long run when we should be tapering! Just allow me to get to that finish line with the ability to still recall my name and, more importantly, where I parked my car.

Runners are also known to be a group willing to go to great lengths if, in return, they have a greater likelihood of remaining injury free. I thought of this one early morning at the local track when I glanced down at my webbed toes and concluded that I'd made my own Faustian froglike bargain. In exchange for the potential for better running form, for building stronger foot muscles, and for less leg discomfort, I was willing to exhibit signs of reverse evolution with an oxymoron on my feet: barefoot shoes.

I would gladly accept the stares, the whispering, and the raised eyebrows from the cotton-hoodies-and-sweatpants crowd circling the track in exchange for my developing better running form. Given that I'd worn socks on my hands (as mittens) in the past, I concluded it wasn't totally incongruous to be wearing these "gloves" on my feet.

I had previously read articles on the benefits of barefoot running: better biomechanics, elimination of injuries, a natural gait with more forefoot and midfoot landing (versus heel striking), improved balance, and a gentler, springier stride. As I stood on the soft and spongy track, I was fully aware that the proponents of barefoot running say there's no discomfort to your feet sprinting along on asphalt, concrete, or cobblestone streets. But the idea of running on my local roads sans shoes wasn't something I was itching to lace them up for. Err, I mean not lace them up for. As for me, I wasn't yet planning to have my toad feet be my road feet.

There are certainly different opinions on the pros and cons of barefoot running and, in the end, it's figuring out what works best for you. But whichever side of the foot you're on, there's consensus that shoe companies have definitely taken notice. One size doesn't fit all, though, and there will be those who may benefit by going completely barefoot and those who do better with a bit more protection through something like the barefoot-like shoe. Other runners will find that wearing more traditional running shoes (with greater motion control and padding) enables their leg muscles to feel the best. Their motto could be "What's good for the shod is good for the quad."

Modification of the barefoot running philosophy in some camps has recently occurred. Some feel that it isn't so much the shoes versus no-shoes approach, but rather the manner in which we run that mitigates injury and enables us to run more efficiently. Form over *dys*function. It's kind of like the old saying that you can put lipstick on a pig, but it's still a pig. With some runners you can take the shoe off a foot, but it's still a heel striker!

Some people believe that it's easier to avoid heel striking when running barefoot or with shoes with a heel that isn't built up. In attempting to reach middle ground, shoe companies began producing minimalist shoes. Not quite barefoot, but not controlling the natural movement of the foot. The less-is-more approach. The minimalist shoe theory holds that the more your foot is allowed to move naturally (closer to barefoot) the more likely it is that your form will improve to its most efficient level. Minimalist shoes provide less cushioning, no motion control, and minimal to low heel height—but what's less and what's too low is particular to the individual. There are those who will still dare to go bare, but with respect to shoes, I remain in the camp of care to still wear.

However, I was willing to try the less-is-more approach. Having recently completed a video gait analysis with recommendations for improving my form, I bought (along with my glovelike "shoe") a pair of minimalist shoes. Interestingly, many of the shoes I looked at were remarkably similar to my shoes when I began running back in the 1970s. What's old is new again. Or more specifically, what's being sold is less shoe again.

The shoes I purchased were what I'd call minimally minimal (my technical term). They weren't the extreme minimal just-above-barefoot model, but they did have a relatively low heel-to-toe ratio (designed to make it easier to achieve the more natural midfoot or forefoot landing), weighed less than a handful of paperclips, and, by design, offered little support, cushioning, or stability. I'd never been so excited to pay more to receive less. Go figure.

As with most things, everything is best in moderation. Of course, that leads to another running-related oxymoron along with barefoot shoe: moderate runner. Often, with a runner, excessive is thy middle name. If you tell runners that barefoot running is great, a large percentage will immediately head off down the pavement without shoes for a quick 10 miler to see how it feels. However, with the transition to running in less shoe, it's recommended to proceed cautiously, incorporate form and foot-strengthening drills, and stretch calves and hamstrings. In the end, the goal is to determine exactly what works best for your foot. Which is what I did in finding that at certain times a minimalist shoe was best and at other times a more traditional shoe was, and form drills worked great while wearing the frog feet.

And with my new shoe wardrobe, I could elect to go as Web-Toed Salamander Man for Halloween next year. I'll have a leg up by already having the feet part down.

Rhythm of the Run

There will be
"Dancing in the Street"

I am a coordination contradiction in motion. Sportswise, I was blessed with better-than-average abilities and could always catch a football, shoot a basketball, or hit a baseball. That is simply the luck of the draw. However, certain other activities requiring elements of coordination have escaped my synapses although not deterred my determination. That is more the pluck of the flaw.

My coordination contradiction is quite evident in the activity of dancing. One would think that my relative smoothness on the basketball floor would flow to the dance floor as well. However, my ability to coordinate dance moves is a bit frightful. I display the grace of a short-circuiting jackhammer on the dance floor. I'm pretty much incapable of coordinating hand clapping if I have to toss in the movement of a leg at the same time. My version of swing dance often devolves into fling dance, and I once unintentionally disengaged my wife from my arm and abruptly threw her into the band at a high rate of speed.

My woeful dance abilities popped into my head when I began reading about the necessity of running with good cadence and rhythm, maintaining an appropriate number of strides per minute, and counting steps. Cadence and steps brought back memories of dancing, where my rhythm was fairly consistent with that of an overly caffeinated three-legged hyena.

Certainly, I had a bit of flow with my running and could sometimes feel quite nimble and fluid. I also knew that how I felt and how I appeared to others were often two different things. This was similar to my once believing I could shuffle step with the gracefulness of Fred Astaire, only to be advised it was more like the gawkiness of Fred Flintstone.

Running does have its own version of the shuffle step. Many running coaches and experts are advising runners to use a more efficient short stride with their legs landing under their hips or their center of gravity (instead of overstriding and landing with an ineffective heel strike). My dance shuffle may look like my feet are engaged in their own internal scuffle, but I figured I could do a decent version of the quick-paced running shuffle. The latter isn't the stiff-legged plodding motion of Frankenstein's monster, but one with a bend to the knees and a circular motion to the legs as they cycle down the road. The general consensus is that you should strive for 170 to 180 strides per minute, although the exact number may vary from runner to runner. Like a good dance partner, shorter strides and greater frequency go hand in hand (or better yet, foot in foot) with achieving speed and also assist in creating a more productive foot strike. The clincher is being able to lengthen your stride while also maintaining a quick stride rate because stride length and frequency equals speed. Not exactly the rocket science of quantum physics and E equals MC squared, but a formula basic enough for even me to grasp.

Many people suggest that a metronome, used by musicians to keep the beat and maintain a constant tempo, is useful in increasing one's strides per minute and establishing a good cadence. I foresaw that establishing running cadence to the beat of a metronome would be as difficult for me as mastering the steps to the popular line dance to Stevie Wonder's, "My Eyes Don't Cry." In that dance, I was always the guy going left while everyone was going right, bending forward while everyone else was moving back, turning outside instead of inside. My song was more "Your Eyes Will Cry" from laughter when watching me. I can't even dance to the beat of my own drummer!

The key now, though, with respect to stride rate and the ping of my running metronome, was being able to dance to the beat of my inner runner. I remained less than optimistic that I'd find success in achieving the rhythm of the run with my mechanical beeping dance partner.

The good news was that this partner wouldn't have to stifle laughter. I foresaw myself concentrating so hard on having my feet land in conjunction with the beeping of the metronome that I'd lose focus on some of the other key components of successful running. Like breathing.

I initially found it incredibly awkward to run according to the sound of the metronome emanating from my waistband. This was even though I started slowly and not overly ambitious. Billy Ray Cyrus's "Achy Breaky Heart" may have produced smooth dance steps, but my awkward movements during my initial metronome runs was more like "Herky Jerky Legs." The rhythm of the run was more like the jarring of the jog.

Over time I got used to the metronome, and my stride rate and cadence improved considerably. I ultimately abandoned my beeping partner but not before recognizing that it helped me to run faster while avoiding heel striking and generating less ground impact. It also helped with my endurance because it felt like I needed to use less energy. The even better news in mastering the metronome is that I think it also helped a little with my dancing ability.

I admit that I'm still incapable of smoothly performing The Hustle on the dance floor, but at least it no longer appears I'm engaged in The Tussle with my appendages. And with my new efficient, short stride with a higher frequency, I'm now the fastest forward stepper on the dance floor. Unfortunately no awards are given to the one who finishes the dance before everyone else and halfway through the song.

I'm still working on my ability to bust a move on the dance floor. But at least while running, I've now got my groove.

CHAPTER 39

Getting the Bends for Bending

Can a runner with the flexibility of concrete survive yoga?

"You're going to a yogurt class?" my young daughter asked me as I grabbed one of her gymnastics mats.

She had the class part right, but this was more popular culture than bacterial culture. I advised her that I was actually going to my first yoga class. I'd finally given in to all the articles I'd read in the running magazines espousing the benefits of yoga for runners. I was indeed a bit late in bending onboard the yoga bandwagon. Many of my friends swore by the benefits of yoga, and studios continued to seemingly pop up on every block. I ultimately became convinced that yoga was not a here today, gone tomorrow pop culture fad. Given that it's been around a wee bit of time, say about 5,000 years, it's lasted slightly longer than the passing fitness fancy of weighted hula hoops and pole dancing workouts.

My young daughter was probably better suited for yoga than I was because children her age appear to have the flexibility of a garden hose. On the other side of the hamstring stretch, the combination of 40-plus years of running and inadequate stretching have left me about as limber as wooden broom handle. The yoga articles I'd read discussed how running provided too much pounding, tightening, and shortening of the muscles and not enough restorative, elongating, and loosening work, the latter of which yoga could provide. My elongating and loosening goal, many yoga classes down the path to enlightenment, was to actually gain the ability to sit cross-legged without needing the assistance of a hoist to rise from the floor. Hey, you have your definition of achievement and I'll have mine.

I'd also read about how yoga creates balance within the body while strengthening all muscle groups that support the skeletal system and also bringing the brain and body together, producing a feeling similar to a runner's high. I was hoping to avoid producing a yoga low, such as the instructor having to roll me back to my car like some giant twisted human pretzel after my rigid body became inexorably wedged into a particular pose.

Days earlier I had called a local yoga studio and inquired whether they offered a prebeginner class for those, like me, whose last 15-second pose was sitting for their sixth-grade school picture. A pleasant woman assured me I'd be fine if, when attempting the different poses, I remembered to honor my body and not do anything that was too discomforting. I replied that if I truly honored my body, I'd wait in the lobby with some green tea while others engaged in their Zen limits of body bending. She had obviously not been privy to obsessed distance runners whose mantra hovers closer to "Abuse my body." I've been known to try to run through a case of plantar fasciitis for nine months, which turned

> Days earlier I had called a local yoga studio and inquired whether there was a prebeginner class for those, like me, whose last 15-second pose was sitting for their sixth grade school picture.

out to be a less-than stellar-approach to avoiding anything too discomforting.

Before the class began I was slightly intimidated by the photographs on the studio walls depicting the poses of people who seemed to be direct descendants of rubber bands. The class started with everyone lying on their respective mats and concentrating on relaxation. Within 14 seconds I was asleep. I was awakened by a soft kick from the instructor, who was advising the class how we needed to concentrate on posture, rhythmic breathing, and limb placement. Since I often have difficulty doing just one thing at a time, I figured as long as I accomplished the goal of staying on my mat for the entire class then things were going well.

After initial relaxation exercises, we did a Seated Forward Bend, otherwise known as the Intense Stretch of the West. Coincidentally, that's what I call the last six miles of my hit-the-wall experience years ago at the San Francisco Marathon. The instructor assured us that it didn't matter whether we could grab our toes or only our ankles in this pose. I was struggling to reach my shins and remain on my mat without falling over.

> The class started with everyone lying on their respective mats and concentrating on relaxation. Within 14 seconds I was asleep.

We did more poses and while almost everyone else was able to do the Half Lord of the Fishes pose, I could only tremble at the thought of what the Full Lord required. Eventually, the class wound down with the Downward Facing Dog pose. This was designed to elongate and strengthen my back and stimulate my brain while improving memory and concentration. I could always use assistance in remembering to concentrate.

Then something unanticipated occurred. There it was, completely out of the blue. A droplet hit my mat, and at first I thought the roof was leaking but then realized that it was sweat.

My sweat. Lo and behold, this wasn't just a supplement to my stretching routine (okay, full disclosure, one actually needs a routine to be able to supplement it), this was a decent workout in and of itself as we quickly went from one pose to the next.

I did indeed enjoy the class and afterward was more than ecstatic in concluding there was no need for anyone to roll me limb-locked back to the car. Equally important, I never fell over and thus avoided turning yoga into a contact sport with my classmates on the mats next to me.

If I stuck with yoga I knew I could lessen the physical impact of running on my body, which would hopefully translate to less injury and faster race times. I even became confident of eventually touching my toes in the Paschimottanasana position or at least being able to efficiently use that word in my next Hanging With Friends game.

And if you happen to see me after a run in a Happy Baby Pose, well, you'll know I'd had a good run.

PART

XI

Behind Every Runner Are Very Accepting Nonrunners

The Runner's Family Knows Their RICE From Their DOMS

For Better or for Worse

A union of soles and souls

I've been a runner for as long as I can remember. Admittedly, with my aging memory, some may not think that's such a remarkable feat of the feet given I have a hard enough time even recalling the course I ran this morning.

Nonetheless, I do actually have a distant recollection of the beginning of my running addiction. I was 11 years old at summer camp and ran early each morning with my counselors, who were 10 years older than me. I did my best to keep up with them while they did their best to filter their comments regarding the female counselors. It probably helped me keep pace by knowing they could slip up at any moment and offer some lascivious commentary. Obviously, the highlight of the day (if not the summer) for a preteen boy.

There's only one thing I've been committed to almost as long as running. The one thing that requires similar traits of dedication and effort and which also produces great happiness: (not to sound overly schmaltzy) my marriage. Now I know some people negatively view matrimony and use "the old ball and chain" terminology, and some runners view marathons as "the old wall and pain." But running and marriage can both produce harmonious results, and with the latter you don't incur the risk of depleting your glycogen reserves in the process. Well, at least I don't.

The comparisons between running and my marriage are manifold, with each having provided an incredible number of wonderful highlights and a smattering of unavoidable lowlights tossed in along the way. Both realms have also brought me plenty of those "What was I thinking?" moments. In running, I've questioned my decision to race a marathon with wind chill readings well below zero that left me feeling like a frozen and rusty tin man. I've also imprudently tried to run through a painful ankle issue only to produce a swollen lower leg the size of a large cantaloupe. My moments of folly within my marriage include obliviously and rapidly backing my car out of the garage directly into my wife's vehicle, which was parked in the driveway. I thus confirmed the accuracy of the old adage that most accidents happen close to home, although I'm thinking that saying wasn't necessarily referring to 54 inches from the home.

Despite my blunders in the realms of running and marriage, I've gained enough knowledge to conclude that the attributes and learning that produce success in running are also the same ones that produce a successful marriage or relationship. At least with me they are. Although some lessons take a bit longer to learn than others because at times my antennae don't pick up all the channels. But I ultimately get a connection, as static as that may be at times.

The beauty of running is its basic cause-and-effect relationship. If you want to run faster or farther or both, you need to train more by increasing your mileage or adding more diligent speed work or both. You're in con-

> Although some lessons take a bit longer to learn than others because at times my antennae don't pick up all the channels. But I ultimately get a connection, as static as that may be at times.

trol. American running great and Olympian Desiree Davila said it well in an article by Jo-Ann Barnas in the Jan. 12, 2012, issue of the *Detroit Free Press* when she talked about Brian Sell's strong third-place performance at the 2008 men's Olympic Marathon Trials:

> Because he was prepared, he didn't have to do anything different or special, or have this magical day," Davila said. "That's running. There's all these things in life, and you don't know why they happen the way they do. But running isn't like that. It's so simple: You put in what you want to put in, and at the end of the day, you get the result you earn. You can't deceive yourself. It's the weird way of finding truth.

Now I'm not a marriage expert. I only have my experience to draw from, but I'd say producing a successful relationship also stems from putting in the required effort.

Similarities abound between running and a great relationship. I'm not equating the latter to those less-than-stellar running experiences where your legs feel like loose jelly and your head is spinning like you just got off a lengthy turn on the Mad Tea Party ride at Disney World. Rather, I'm talking about those times when everything clicks, you feel like you're effortlessly gliding along with your feet barely touching the ground, and you're light as a feather. Nirvana on the roads.

On a recent long run I thought of the similar traits required to produce a great running performance as well as a happy marriage (at least for my marriage). If you plug the concept of relationship or marriage within the context of running as stated here, the similarities are readily apparent:

> From the beginning of training for long-distance running, you need to have **respect** for what you'll undertake and be **attentive** to detail to achieve success. You'll head for heartbreak city if you think things will go well by simply showing up and without putting in the required **effort**.

You have to **trust** your training and recognize that if you sufficiently **work at it** and have a strong **commitment**, you will be rewarded with a remarkably enjoyable and successful experience. You have to love it, though, because there is not much point in plodding onward if the love for running is gone and no longer gratifying.

Communication between you and your running is critical: You **need to listen** to your body during training. You need to know when to back off when a sign of potential injury or problem arises and to **immediately address issues before they become something more significant**.

You need to be **faithful** to your running and not be swayed by the sleek and shiny exercise machines, which may momentarily attract you. They won't lead you into greater happiness or race times. Your **loyalty** to running will be rewarded in kind.

If you give to running, then running will give back to you. **Don't take it for granted**, though. **Appreciate** it always because you never know when things like an injury will arise and running will not be there for a while.

Every now and then your running may feel flat. At that point, you need to shake things up, **experience new things together**, and be more **innovative** and **spontaneous** with your running. You may have to instill a spark by hitting the trails instead of the roads, changing your pace, or running at a different time than usual. Do **fun things together**, explore new areas to run, **travel together** to new places.

You need to have **realistic expectations** to achieve obtainable goals in your running. Have **patience** with training and know that **daily attention** to all things running will inevitably produce the results you're after. Exhibit **acceptance** as well, given that not every day will feel magical but usually something good will come from each run.

Learn from your experiences so that you don't repeat training mistakes. If you want your running to improve and be strong, you must be willing to make **compromises** and **sacrifices**. You'll need to **work together** with your running to resolve difficulties that may arise in your training and determine what works best.

Be kind to your running and it will be kind to you, but if you mistreat it through things like overtraining, then you'll pay the price. It's not necessarily the number of miles you run or the quantity of time you put in. Instead, what produces successful running is the **quantity of the quality**.

You need to pay **attention to the little things** to experience success as a runner. These include postrun nutrition and recovery, muscle massage, and hydration. As you grow together over the years, you'll need to **make adjustments** in your running and determine what works best.

Perhaps the greatest thing that running and a marriage have in common is that when that alarm goes off early in the morning to get you up for a run, you know you've got two great friends. One's willing to take you down the road and enable you to feel the terrain under your feet and alive with energy. Admittedly, the other may simply roll over in bed, pull the covers up, and go back to sleep while awaiting your return.

But they will both always be there for you when you need them.

Over Hill, Over Dale, and I'm Pale

Does the mud bath cost extra?

At a certain stage of a running career, one may find that a traditional 10K, half- or full-marathon race on a relatively flat asphalt course begins to fall into the "been there, done that" category of life. At least it did for me when I began to seek different types of races that broke from the traditional courses and distances.

A friend told me about the Rectifier Run in Montague, Michigan, which was a completely off-road European cross country–style event with hay bales and logs and other hurdles to leap. It was also spiced with mud pools to wade through. Not your run-of-the-mill Saturday-morning race but more a run where you might fall on your face.

I described the event to my 11-year-old son and he was geeked, although I'm sure that just a fleeting reference to a mud pool would have been compelling enough for him. Despite my concern that I hadn't hurdled anything in years higher than a 3 × 5 index card, we registered. Race day arrived and the first things I noticed in walking to the course were outdoor showers and a slew of thigh-deep, water-filled bins scattered about the finish area. We were clearly in for a unique race. If you were handicapping the run like a horserace, you'd want to know which racers were the true mudders. I don't mean the runners who can find good treading and balance in fairly wet dirt, but those who can quickly get through a thick, black quicksand-type lagoon with their femurs still remaining in their hip sockets.

The indications that the race would be different continued when the race director offered a few short words. Instead of the typical and initial welcoming of runners, the race director asked the crowd, "If anyone is the type to litigate if he or she gets injured, well, could you please leave now?"

> I don't mean the runners who can find good treading and balance in fairly wet dirt, but those who can quickly get through a thick, black quicksand-type lagoon with their femurs still remaining in their hip sockets.

Those weren't the most comforting prerace words I would have liked to hear. The starting gun went off just as my son was asking, "What is *lit a gate*?" I'm sure he was excitedly thinking that around the bend was the opportunity to jump over flaming fences like an outdoor Cirque du Soleil.

At first, things seemed easy enough. The initial hurdle was just a little foot-high log jump. Despite having a quarter-mile running start, I cleared it with only half a centimeter to spare. I'm not sure whether my hop-along son even noticed it existed; he never broke stride.

The degree of difficulty of the barriers quickly changed, and we encountered monstrous (to me at least) sand piles, log jumps, hay bales, and so on. (You non-Rectifier runners have no clue what *and so on* means. To participate is to know.) Word of warning if you're someone who tends to zone out during races: You may find yourself firmly planted, forehead first, in a suddenly appearing 10-foot-high hard mound of dirt. All of which gives new meaning to hitting the wall.

My son had a continuous ear-to-ear smile on his face, while I'm sure I was exuding a look of sheer fear, not knowing whether the mother of all obstacles was lurking ahead of us.

As we ran through a barn during the latter portion of the race, I could tell we were approaching the legendary mud pond when we began to hear the squeals of spectators and runners alike. Soon we rounded a corner and headed toward the sludge-and-muck pool of yuck. I initially wondered whether our shoes would have to be totaled after the race. But upon wading into the mud, which was well near waist high, it became a nonissue because our shoes were quickly separated from our feet. I was silently praying my ankles didn't detach as well.

Not knowing whether the lagoon would swallow my son, I gallantly allowed him to climb on my shoulders. We were eventually able to extricate ourselves from the morass, and I was thankful I wouldn't have to explain to my wife how 12 strangers and a mule were required to remove us from the quagmire.

Covered in mud, we slowly moved toward the finish line together. My son was in seventh heaven as he enthusiastically hollered along with the other runners and spectators. Despite the fact that the inherent enthusiasm of an 11-year-old boy is usually quite contagious, I remained more solemn. I was more than a bit concerned that somewhere under the mud encasing my body existed the likelihood that my running shorts had come off as well. Once we finished, I quickly hopped in the outdoor shower to face the inevitable. Twenty minutes of mud washing later, I was able to discern that, thankfully for all, my shorts had remained in place.

As we headed back to the car, my son was already asking whether we could sign up for next year's race. I only hoped that by then I would have successfully removed all the dried mud from my eyelashes and ears.

Of course, as any competitive runner would do, I started devising training methods to improve my race time. It appeared that to simulate the thick and deep mud pool, knee-high snowdrift wind sprints were going to be on next winter's training regimen.

Bring on that mire! No stick in the mud for me.

Have Shoes, Will Travel

Maintaining marital bliss on race-destination vacations

I have always been uncertain of the accuracy of the phrase "opposites attract." In my track and field and running world, I thought that if the phrase were true, I'd probably marry a high jumper since I need a running start and a mini-trampoline to successfully leap over a step stool.

I actually wound up going further down the line of opposing athletic personalities: I fell in love with—dare I even say it—a nonrunner. Talk about your interfaith marriages. Truth be told, my lovely wife was a recreational runner when we first met. However, a few years later she set a personal record in the 10K at 21 years of age, and thereafter, she unceremoniously exited the world of bruised toenails and periodic shin splints. She claimed something about wanting to go out on top.

I held out hope that she would see the light and reemerge from the nonimpact forms of exercise she'd substituted for running. I dreamed of becoming her supporter and coach and pacing her at an exciting race in an attractive city as we finished her first marathon together. But after 25-plus years of marriage and with her dust-laden running log stuck at zero, I've given up all hope that the romantic bond of our sharing an energy gel packet at mile 22 is in our foreseeable future.

One of the inherent problems with the merging of a runner and a nonrunner is vacationing. A vacation involving a race is an oxymoron to a nonrunner. My wife and I have visited many lovely places for races: Bermuda, Boston, Seattle, San Francisco, Denver, and New York City. I feel at home among my running brethren in moisture-wicking clothing, and my sightseeing tour of the city is always accomplished by participating in the race. On the other side of the starting line, it's safe to say my wife has failed to grasp the inherent joy of standing in a 10-row-deep crowd of spectators on an unseasonably cold and rainy October morning with a 50-50 chance of actually locating me as thousands of runners zip by. My sharing with her the postrace refreshments of a plain bagel, half a banana, and lukewarm sport drink doesn't meet her expectations of a deliciously satisfying breakfast.

But after 25-plus years of marriage and with her dust-laden running log stuck at zero, I've given up all hope that the romantic bond of our sharing an energy gel packet at mile 22 is in our foreseeable future.

Many years ago my wife began to understand the drawbacks of running vacations when I tried to convince her that one of the highlights of an upcoming trip would be the unlimited garlic bread and three types of pasta sauce at the prerace dinner. At that point, she was a wee bit hesitant to ask about my other anticipated highlights. She'd been thinking more along the lines of a romantic dinner followed by a leisurely walk to a chic dessert shop and finishing the evening at a trendy jazz bar. Instead, I was offering half-hour lines at the pasta buffet in the cacophony of an undersized banquet room surrounded by thousands of nervously chattering runners and a dessert selection usually limited to semistale peanut butter cookies. Needless to say, we didn't possess the same travel agent.

And a postdinner romantic stroll? Sacrilege! Not happening because I am convinced that any extra steps on my feet the night before a race equate to crucial seconds added to my race finishing time. I'm prone as soon as possible after the last strand of spaghetti is formally sucked into my carbo-loaded stomach. I then plant myself in front of the hotel room television and hope that *Chariots of Fire* is included in the movie offerings.

I recall a trip to Manhattan some years back for the New York City Marathon. My wife envisioned attending a Broadway play followed by a late-night dinner, shopping along Fifth Avenue, an afternoon of touring museums, and tossing in a walk across the Brooklyn Bridge. The only bridge I was crossing was the Verrazano at the start of the race, while my afternoon tour would be of the race expo collecting souvenir headbands and sampling bite-size offerings of free energy bars. My time on Fifth Avenue would be as I hit mile 21 of the race and then going through East Harlem.

After a few race trips together, I assured my wife that if she'd tolerate my idiosyncrasies the day before a race, I'd be available afterward to do all she wanted to do in exploring a new city. Sounds good in theory, but not so much in reality. The truth is my postrace activities are usually hampered by an inability to walk more than 10 yard stretches at a shuffling pace before having to stop to readjust the bandages on my blistered toes.

But, as it does in any good marriage, the spirit of compromise comes into play. I have no room to complain about touring another art museum on a nonrace vacation. In turn, my wife will politely endure my mile-by-mile rendition of a just-completed race on a race-related trip.

My spirit of compromise has gone so far as agreeing to a prerace shopping excursion as long as it is confined to one store with elevators and those lovely couches outside the dressing rooms that are great for a nice nap. I'm also ready and willing for a trip to a nice dessert shop the evening of a race because I've got plenty of calories to replenish. Admittedly though, my wife has had to wake me up and drag me back to the hotel after I've suddenly nodded off into my tiramisu.

Our research is also a bit different when selecting a vacation spot. My wife looks for sightseeing and adventures, evening entertainment, and tasty restaurant meals. I'm more concerned with whether there are nearby running trails, a well-equipped hotel fitness center, and a local store for purchasing running gear should my luggage get lost in transit.

The fact is, she knew when we first met that I was a runner, although she clearly didn't recognize the depth of eccentricities this would bring to our years together. She's lovingly supported me through bad races, recurring injuries, sleeping with my right shoe on to treat a case of plantar fasciitis, toenail treatments on the family room floor, and a postmarathon hospitalization due to hyponatremia. She's also accepted my ubiquitous wardrobe of running shirts and tolerated a ceiling-high stockpile of boxes of discontinued running shoes decorating our closet. My wife has also endured my lying facedown on the couch at 7:30 p.m. because a long run that morning was suddenly taking its toll.

She's also patiently dealt with my ongoing quest for hydration that finds me with the ever present water bottle, often requiring my use of public restrooms every 40 minutes. My wife has accepted my alarm going off at 3:00 a.m. so I could get a run in before an early-morning plane trip and has also endured way too many postrace award ceremonies that tended to last slightly longer than the Academy Awards Oscar presentations on TV. She's accepted my driving with four pillows on my seat to assist with the discomfort of a bothersome piriformis muscle and that it's best not to talk to me after an

> She's lovingly supported me through bad races, recurring injuries, sleeping with my right shoe on to treat a case of plantar fasciitis, toenail treatments on the family room floor, and a postmarathon hospitalization due to hyponatremia.

exhausting workout because my ability to generate coherent thoughts at that time is nonexistent.

She's also enthusiastically greeted me at finish lines when my race time exceeded expectations, shared in my irrepressible glee over a new running shoe, and helped bring me back from the depths of despair when Murphy's Law of Running conjured an injury right before a much-anticipated race.

The beauty of all this includes the fact that my daughter has also been exposed to my peculiarities, and should she marry a runner, she will be well adapted to the quirks of her husband. I recall years ago arriving early at school to pick up my daughter from fifth grade. To pass the time, I exited my car and engaged in a series of enthusiastic stretches on the front lawn of the school. Unbeknown to me, my daughter had a window seat in her classroom to witness my activity. When she came out of school, after having apparently viewed my impromptu stretching routine with much embarrassment, all she could muster was an exasperated, "Really, Dad? Really?"

Unapologetically, I replied with a smile and said, "Yeah, really, dear. Can't help myself. Go talk to your mom. She'll explain."

Appendix

What Color Is Your Singlet?

Do you know your lactate from your pronate? Your swing gait from your heart rate?

Cool down by taking the runner's quotient exam.

I have never been a fan of those lists that begin with "You know you're a [fill in the blank] if you . . ." The lists were getting a bit too specific with titles such as "You know you're a conservative-leaning Northeasterner who loves food reality shows, indie folk music, baba ghanoush, and Scrabble if you . . ."

Plenty of lists address "You know you're a runner if you . . ." I try to cast a larger net and include everyone from the competitive female 50K runner to the 5K guy in cotton socks and a cutoff sweatshirt within my definition of runner. I figure if you golf, you're a golfer, if you shoot skeet, you're a skeet shooter, and if you run, you're a runner. But if you're a golfing, skeet-shooting runner, well then I'm not sure what you are.

Runners come in various types, and that's no truer than nowadays. I admit to being one of those old-school runners who didn't initially welcome the more recent running boom. The first running boom in the 1970s (which I admit to being a part of) brought runners forth from the darkness and included large doses of obsessive and eccentric behavior along with a competitively hard-core approach to running. Fitness was a byproduct and not a focus. We were viewed as being on the fringe, if not a tad unhinged.

The recent running boom is a democratization of running into a large social activity. It's more low key, mainstream, and inclusive, and runners come in all shapes and sizes. There's a different mindset. Many newer runners are more interested in the goal of completing a race and less concerned about competing for time. There's more focus on fitness and participation than speed, and there also has been a large influx of women into the running world. Over time, I changed my tune and welcomed the mass of participants into "my" sport. I came around to the view that everyone can approach running and enjoy it on any level they may desire. The more people who run and improve their physical and mental health is all the better. The larger number of runners is great and helps to keep the sport alive and lively (although I'm still getting used to race course entertainment including acrobats, belly dancers, Latin drums, Ukrainian Cossack dancers, and Croatian folk bands).

All this said, the following runner's quotient (R.Q.) test is designed to illustrate the types of runners in our sport. There are no right or wrong answers, so just enjoy taking the quiz and see what category of runner you fall into. As with today's approach to running, all who participate are winners. (No finisher medals, though.)

If you'd like to print out the test before taking it, go to www.runninglaughsblog.com and click the link for the Runner's Quotient Test.

R.Q. Test

Scoring:

One point for A

Two points for B

Three points for C

Four points for D (and no need to Google until the quiz has been completed)

No points if none of the answers applies to you.

Extra-point questions are worth a single point.

Choose the answer that best applies to you:

1. When you meet someone for the first time who appears to be a runner, you:
    A. Don't ever think about who might be a runner because you're a runner who doesn't appear to be a runner
    B. Look to see whether he or she is wearing running shoes
    C. And then look to see whether the person is wearing a running watch
    D. And then hope he or she first asks you whether you're a runner

2. You've been to a track:
    A. Because you were there to watch a high school football game or the band
    B. To run laps so you know how far you went
    C. To do a workout, but your speed work is predominately done on the roads and trails
    D. Weekly during racing season, and you often do at least 10 Yasso 800s[1]

3. When a running injury may have emerged during a run, you:
    A. Schedule a doctor's appointment within one hour after the run

---

[1] 800 meter repeats. Average 800 times can predict upcoming marathon time (i.e. 3 minute 10 second 800 time equals a 3 hour 10 minute marathon).

    B. Decide to take a week off and see how it responds to rest

    C. Elect to rest from running but first determine which cross-training option will not aggravate the pain

    D. Ignore the pain and load up on ibuprofen and run, limp, or crawl through the injury for at least three months before ultimately seeing a doctor

    E. **Extra point**: Continue "running" to near the date of the doctor's appointment and cancel at least once before finally going.

4. When a running magazine arrives with its seasonal review of new shoes, you:

    A. Put it aside to peruse at your leisure

    B. Thumb through it to see the latest shoe colors and designs

    C. Experience a faster heart rate and sweating palms, and you immediately read it in its entirety

    D. Don't bother reading it because you've already researched upcoming shoes in depth online, printed out the information, and have calendared the release dates of two or more models

    E. **Zero points:** You don't subscribe to a running magazine

5. In your house you have:

    A. A framed picture of yourself during or after a race

    B. At least one training book

    C. And at least one unopened box of your favorite running shoes

    D. And at least one running-related poster on the wall and a location for old race numbers with your race time written on the back of each number

6. When traveling by airplane, you:

    A. Take no extra precautions with your running shoes and clothing

    B. Make sure you don't pack your running shoes within checked luggage

C. And you also don't pack your running clothing within checked luggage

D. And you also take on board at least two running magazines or a running book to read on the plane and a tennis ball or pillow to sit on should your piriformis act up

7. Your initial thought after completing 20 miles in training (or what would be your thought in the event you haven't yet run 20 miles) is:

A. Dang, I just burned off about 2,000 calories

B. Dang, I'm in pretty good shape

C. Dang, that felt good; maybe I should have tacked on 2 more for 22 miles

D. Dang, I tacked on 2 more and went 22 miles

8. Your dog is (or if you were going to get a dog it would be) named:

A. Max, Charlie, Mollie, Lady or something in that vein

B. Pre

C. Lasse (and there's no misspelling there)[2]

D. Bekele or the name of some other famous east-African runner[3]

9. To you, a ladder:

A. Is something in your garage that takes you to greater heights

B. Involves interval training and takes your heart rate to greater heights

C. And you do them weekly

D. And you've done them on a track, on grass, on a trail, and on the roads[4]

E. **Extra point**: You've shoveled snow off a track to gain access to a clear lane for intervals or ran track intervals during a thunderstorm.

---

[2] Finnish distance runner Lasse Viren (winner of 4 Olympic gold medals).
[3] Ethiopian distance runner Kenenisa Bekele (world record holder in 5,000 and 10,000 and gold medal winner).
[4] Ladders are a series of increasing and decreasing intervals separated by periods of recovery.

10. To you, the name Jack Daniels means:

    A. A type of whiskey

    B. One of the greatest running coaches and exercise physiologists

    C. The author of *Daniels's Running Formula*, which you've read

    D. And you also know he's an Olympian in the modern pentathlon and coached SUNY Cortland to eight NCAA titles

11. You have:

    A. Never urinated anyplace other than an indoor bathroom

    B. Urinated in a prerace Porta-Potty

    C. Urinated somewhere else outside when the Porta-Potty lines were too long

    D. Urinated on yourself during a race so as not to waste time stopping

12. With respect to the city considered Track Town in the United States:

    A. You have no idea why there'd even be a Track Town

    B. You thought it was Indy for the Indianapolis Speedway

    C. You know it is Eugene, Oregon, but only from watching movies on Steve Prefontaine

    D. You know of former U of O runners Nicole Blood, Kenny Moore, Joaquim Cruz, and Mac Wilkins (but you can't recall your congressman's name or the secretary of the treasury)

    E. **Extra point:** You know the significance of the ROTC drill scene in the 1978 movie *Animal House*.[5]

13. The outside of your car has:

    A. A bumper sticker saying 13.1

    B. A bumper sticker saying 26.2

    C. A bumper sticker saying 26.3 (these humorous ones exist)

    D. No bumper stickers because you feel no need to display what distances you've run

---

[5] Hayward Field is seen in background of the movie, filmed in Eugene.

14. With respect to Haile Gebrselassie, you know:

    A. Nothing because the only Haile you know is Halle Berry

    B. That he's a runner

    C. And what country he's from and his nickname and knew how to correctly spell his last name

    D. And know the distances of at least four of the world records he has held[6]

    E. **Extra point**: You have seen his biographical movie *Endurance*.

15. You know who the following female runners are:

    A. Oprah Winfrey (at least in 1994 she was a runner when she completed her only marathon)

    B. Kara Goucher[7] and Shalane Flanagan

    C. Desiree Davila[8]

    D. Ingrid Kristiansen, Paula Radcliffe, and Grete Waitz[9]

    E. **Extra point:** Lynn Jennings[10]

16. To you, repeats mean:

    A. Television shows

    B. What happens after a spicy Mexican meal

    C. A type of interval training

    D. And you've done them after a spicy Mexican meal

17. With respect to food, you:

    A. Have eaten an energy bar and sport drink for breakfast

    B. Have eaten an energy bar or bars and sport drink for breakfast and lunch on the same day

    C. Prefer pieces of frozen energy bars to hard candy

    D. Have done a taste test and analyzed the nutritional content and ingredients of at least 10 types of energy bars

---

[6] Ethiopian runner (one time holder of world records in marathon, half marathon, one hour run, 10 mile, 5,000 meter, 10,000 meter, and 25K).

[7] USA Olympic runner and 2:24:26 marathoner.

[8] USA Olympic runner and second place Boston marathon finisher in 2:22:38.

[9] Kristiansen (1980s Norwegian runner), Paula Radcliffe (English runner, world record holder, marathon and cross country world champion) and Grete Waitz (Norwegian runner and nine-time NYC marathon winner, Olympic gold medalist, and former world record holder).

[10] American distance runner, Olympic medalist, and three-time world cross country winner.

18. When injured, you:
    A. Slowly ride your bike alongside your running group
    B. Take long walks and do a bit of cross-training
    C. Keep perspective and choose one cross-training modality and do it at least five days a week
    D. Become despondent but incorporate two of the following: pool running, elliptical, stair climber, or spinning and cross-train maniacally on a daily basis

19. With respect to your fuel and hydration belt:
    A. It contains sport drink, energy gel, and a phone
    B. It contains only sport drink
    C. It contains only water
    D. You don't own one and instead, the day before a long run, you strategically place gels or drinks or both along your route

20. With respect to the largest hill in your general running area, you:
    A. Only go up it in a car
    B. Only go up it on a bicycle
    C. Run it at least once a week and enjoy the feeling
    D. Know its exact elevation, do weekly hill repeats on it, have given it a name, and know your PR for ascending it

21. With respect to viewing a major marathon streamed online:
    A. You weren't aware they're shown online
    B. You're aware but can't comprehend someone actually watching an entire marathon
    C. You've watched an entire marathon and listened to the race commentators online
    D. You've watched an entire marathon without audio online

22. With respect to a pace chart, you:
    A. Don't own one because your leisurely pace is rarely included in such a chart
    B. Have one in your house
    C. And one in your car

    D. And in your bathroom, kitchen, and on your nightstand, although you rarely need to consult it because you have most distances and paces fully memorized

23. You know what the following abbreviations stand for:

    A. DNF

    B. And MPW

    C. And ITBS

    D. And DMOS, RICE, IAAF, NSAID, AT[11]

24. With respect to the sport of track:

    A. You didn't know there was a sport of track

    B. You watch some events every four years during the Olympics

    C. You know who Henry Rono is and what he did in 1978[12]

    D. And you know the significance of Bislett Stadium and also what Sebastian Coe did in 1979 within a 41-day stretch[13]

25. When you hear the name John Parker, you think:

    A. Is that my neighbor four houses down?

    B. Leader of the minutemen at the Battle of Lexington

    C. Author of famous fictional running book, *Once a Runner*

    D. And can name the book's main character, his fictional college, and his coach's name[14]

    E. **Extra point**: You also know the name of his best friend.[15]

26. With respect to running shoes, you can define the following:

    A. Shoe laces

    B. And pronation and supination

    C. And flex groove

    D. And Cambrelle, bellows tongue, aglet, and compression-molded EVA

---

[11] Did Not Finish, Miles Per Week, Iliotibial Band Syndrome, Delayed Muscle Onset Soreness, Rest Ice Compression Elevation, International Association of Athletics Federation, Non Steroidal Anti-Inflammatory Drug, Anaerobic Threshold.

[12] Kenyan runner who broke four world records in 81 days in 1978.

[13] Track in Norway where 65 world records have been set.

[14] Quenton Cassidy, Bruce Denton, and Southeastern.

[15] Jerry Mizner.

27. Your idea of a great prerace song is:
    A. "Stronger (What Doesn't Kill You)" by Kelly Clarkson
    B. "Lose Yourself" by Eminem
    C. Any song by Led Zeppelin
    D. "Freebird" by Lynyrd Skynyrd

28. Your car:
    A. Is too pristine to carry running-related gear
    B. Contains at least one sport drink or water bottle at all times
    C. And contains The Stick or a foam roller
    D. And contains at least one running magazine, a towel, safety pins for race numbers, petroleum jelly, and a stretching rope

29. During an airport layover, which provides you the only time that day for a run, you:
    A. Go grab a Cinnabon and take a nap
    B. Walk around the concourse to get some form of exercise
    C. Do a slow run inside the concourse to get that running feeling
    D. Run more than five miles around the airport and stop sweating sometime during the next leg of your plane trip
    E. **Extra point**: You check the next flight before going running in case you choose to run longer and are willing to miss your flight's departure time.

30. Before registering for an out-of-town race, you first:
    A. Determine (or already know) how many of your running friends will join you
    B. Determine the finisher medals, course entertainment, and postrace food
    C. Determine the elevation of the course
    D. Read participant comments, check the race-day weather from the past three years, and check the overall and applicable age-division winners for the last five years

E. **Extra point**: You've run a race in nonpeak shape and rather than associating your name with a slower time, you registered under a pseudonym.

31. With respect to runners named Bill, you are familiar with:

    A. Bill Rodgers

    B. And Billy Mills

    C. And Bill Bowerman

    D. And Bill Squires and Bill Dellinger[16]

32. You know that Coos Bay is:

    A. In Oregon

    B. And Steve Prefontaine was born there

    C. And you've seen the films *Without Limits*, *Prefontaine*, and the documentary *Fire on the Track*

    D. And can name the runner who won the gold medal in the 5,000 meters at the 1972 Olympics (where Pre finished fourth).[17]

    E. **Extra point**: You have also seen the movies *On the Edge* and *The Jericho Mile*.

33. In your freezer, you have:

    A. Ice for postrun diet soft drinks

    B. Ice in cups to use on legs after a run

    C. Four or more blue freezer packs for postrun icing

    D. D. Bags of frozen peas for postrun icing

34. When planning vacations:

    A. You don't think much about running because you tend not to run on vacation

    B. You make certain there are nice areas to run in

    C. And you see what scenic trails exist

    D. You see what's there to do after the race because all your vacations are race-destination trips

---

[16] Rodgers: Former American record holder in marathon and four-time Boston Marathon winner; Mills: 1964 Gold Medal 10,000 meters; Bowerman: University of Oregon track and field coach and cofounder of Nike; Dellinger: 3-time Olympian and former track and field coach at University of Oregon.
[17] Lasse Viren.

35. You know the following terms:

    A. Ready, set, go

    B. Lactic acid

    C. $\dot{V}O2max$

    D. And dirty dozen

36. You have run:

    A. On a treadmill

    B. On a treadmill but have done so only during very inclement weather

    C. On a treadmill and have gone longer than 70 minutes

    D. Only outside and believe treadmills are for gerbils

37. When you hear the word Boston, you first equate it with:

    A. The capital of Massachusetts

    B. The Boston Marathon

    C. Your qualifying time for the Boston Marathon

    D. Your memories from previous Boston Marathon races

    E. **Extra point**: You know the names of the two racers in the Duel in the Sun.[18]

38. Regarding female runners who have left their imprint on the sport, you know:

    A. Deena Kastor[19]

    B. And what Joan Benoit (now Samuelson)[20] was the first woman to do

    C. And what Kathrine Switzer[21] first accomplished

    D. And why Nina Kuscsik[22] is in the National Distance Running Hall of Fame

    E. **Extra point**: You knew the Hall of Fame existed.

---

[18] Alberto Salazar, Dick Beardsley (1-2 finishers in riveting 1982 Boston Marathon).

[19] American record holder in marathon and half marathon, bronze medalist 2004.

[20] Gold medal winner of female marathon in 1984, first time marathon distance was included as Olympic event.

[21] Became first woman to run Boston Marathon as numbered entry (1967).

[22] First woman to run NYC marathon, first female winner of Boston Marathon, and instrumental in getting rules changed to allow women to run in national and international marathons.

39. You've read:

    A. *Galloway's Book on Running*

    B. *4 Months to a 4-Hour Marathon* by Kuehls

    C. *Road Racing for Serious Runners* by Pfitzinger and Douglas

    D. *Lore of Running* by Noakes

    E. **Extra point**: You've read and know that most entertaining, enjoyable, well-written book is *I Run, Therefore I Am —NUTS!* (or this sequel to that book), and you don't know why it didn't win the Pulitzer Prize.

    F. **No points**: Never read a running book

40. In regards to negative splits:

    A. You believe it may have something to do with your running shorts.

    B. You know it means your second half of the race is run faster than the first half.

    C. You've attempted to achieve it, but it still remains elusive.

    D. You've achieved it on those rare occasions when you smartly refrained from pounding yourself into the ground the first half of the race.

41. Your longest consecutive running streak is:

    A. One day

    B. One week

    C. One to three months

    D. Seven or more years and you've prevailed through ice storms, the flu, thunderstorms, and injuries

42. When you run alone:

    A. You don't run alone.

    B. You bring along music.

    C. You sometimes bring music, although you feel Henry David Thoreau wouldn't have approved.

    D. You bring along nothing but your thoughts.

Scoring the R.Q. Test

What color is your singlet?

0-66 Points

Crimson camaraderie—You began running as a social activity and enjoy connecting with your running friends, virtually always running with others. You haven't completely bought into the joy of the physical act of running, although you enjoy how you feel after a run (and now and then like the physical nature of your run). It's more often, though, a tolerable act to provide you the extreme joy of a social group. At times you enter races with friends, but you pretty much have one pace for most distances (and races you enter usually have 5,000 or more participants). The idea of speed work is a foreign concept, and you're completion oriented versus time oriented (both in racing and training). Camaraderie is the critical component for you.

67-110 Points

Fuchsia fitness—You are into fitness and likely came from an athletic background. You're into exercising (and have tried various types), being healthy and physically fit, and controlling your weight. You find running provides you the best alternative toward those goals. You enjoy the social nature of running but are fairly committed to staying in shape and run solo at times.

You vary your pace and try to perform speed training (knowing that interval work may burn more calories and fat). You engage in cross-training on nonrunning days. You participate in races and are somewhat competitive but don't overstrain during racing and aren't overly concerned about your time (but certainly cognizant of it).

111-154 Points

Platinum purist—You have a passion for the physical act of running. You love gliding along, communing with nature. You love feeling your feet flowing across the ground and the joy of sweat, effort, speed, and freedom. You enjoy the meditative aspect of running and prefer solo runs but enjoy the social aspect a few times a week. You compete in and enjoy races, as well as pushing yourself to new limits and are willing to tackle new adventures in running, including trail races and ultras. You employ speed work but usually away from the track. Your intensity in training is not primarily driven by competition because you'd challenge yourself with or without races.

155 or More Points

Olive obsessed—You have a bit of a Type A personality and are a hard-core runner and have either run through two running booms or, if younger, have thrown yourself into running with vigor because you enjoy challenges and competition. You may have grown up with the sport or are a late bloomer, but either way you are committed (although your obsessive nature leads some to think you should literally be committed). You love the thrill of competition and use any training-related device that may enhance race performance (heart rate monitors, intricate GPS watches). If you're older, you're into age-graded performances and master's divisions and events. You've raced various distances in races having a large number of participants and others being very small. You likely keep a running log, do weekly speed work, and incorporate hill training. You love running but are equally fueled by a love of competition.

The fact is whatever division you fell into based on your answers, any type of runner is to be commended. Like the Jets in *West Side Story*, we can sing along to the tune of the "Jet Song" but with our own lyrics:

Runner Song

> When you're a runner
> You run all the way
> From your first-ever mile
> To your fast running days
> When you run if you do hit the wall
> There are runners around
> Pick you up if you fall
> You're never alone
> You're always protected
> You run with the brethren
> When friendship's expected
> We're well connected
> You are all set with a capital R
> Which you'll never forget till your last running day
> When you're a runner, you run all the way.

About the Author and Illustrator

Bob Schwartz is the author of five books, including the highly successful and humorous *I Run, Therefore I Am—NUTS!*, and a freelance writer whose popular articles have been published in over 200 magazines. His humorous essays on running have appeared in more than 40 national and international running magazines and regional magazines, including *Runner's World* and *Running Fitness*.

Bob's books have been finalists in the humor category of the USA Book News Awards, the ForeWord Book Awards, the Benjamin Franklin Book Awards, and the Independent Publisher Book Awards. Bob has also won the Gold Award from the Parenting Publications of America for his humorous essays on family life. Bob has presented humorous talks at races throughout the United States.

Bob lives in Huntington Woods, Michigan, with his wife, Robin, and three children. He graduated from the University of Colorado and received his law degree from the University of Oregon. In addition to his writing, he is the CEO of the Here to Help Foundation (www.heretohelpfoundation.org), which he operates with his wife.

Bob raised over $50,000 through an ultramarathon benefiting the Institute of Craniofacial Surgery and Reconstructive Surgery and received the Dove Award from The Arc for implementing a basketball program for people with physical and mental disabilities. Bob also received the Avadenka Award from the State Bar of Michigan for his community service. He founded the Cheetahs Running Club in the Berkley School District of Michigan, for which he was awarded a grant from the Saucony Run for Good Foundation.

In the universal language of runners, Bob has PRs of 2:42:13 for the marathon, 34:18 for the 10K, 1:16:08 for the half marathon, and 58 seconds for the third-grade potato sack race. You can reach Bob at bob@runninglaughs.com and enjoy his website and follow his blog at www.runninglaughsblog.com. Also, catch Bob on Facebook at www.facebook.com/runninglaughs and on Twitter at @RunningLaughs for daily humor and running news.

B.K. Taylor is a well-known illustrator and writer. He has contributed to such varied media as the National Lampoon, Walt Disney Productions, Jim Henson Productions, MAD, Nickelodeon, Sesame Street and Tim Allen's Home Improvement for ABC (staff writer)

Taylor's work has been recognized with the Inkpot Award, the Gold Brick, seven Caddies, the Funny Bone Award, the Ace Award and the 2010 Reed Award for political cartooning. Taylor lives in Franklin, Michigan, with his wife, Kathleen, and two daughters. His leisure activities include art collecting, traveling, and watching Bob Schwartz run by his studio window.